Lonely Planet

POCKET

AUCKLAND
& THE BAY OF ISLANDS

TOP SIGHTS • LOCAL EXPERIENCES

BRETT ATKINSON, TASMIN WABY

Contents

Plan Your Trip

Welcome to Auckland 4

Top Sights 6

Eating 10

Drinking & Nightlife 12

Shopping............................14

Beaches 16

Māori Culture 17

For Kids 18

Volcanoes 19

History 20

Activities 21

Four Perfect Days 22

Need to Know 24

Auckland Neighbourhoods 26

Māori dance performance on Waitangi Day
CHAMELEONSEYE/SHUTTERSTOCK ©

Explore Auckland 29

City Centre & Britomart ... 31
Viaduct Harbour
& Wynyard Quarter.......... 49
Kingsland & Mt Eden 59
Parnell & Newmarket 69
Ponsonby &
Karangahape Road 83
Waiheke Island 97

Explore the
Bay of Islands 117

Paihia................................... 119
Russell................................. 129
Kerikeri............................... 137

Worth a Trip

Great Barrier Island........ 104
West Auckland 110

Survival Guide 145

Before You Go 146
Arriving in Auckland........ 147
Getting Around 148
Essential Information ... 149
Index.................................... 155

Special Features

Auckland Art Gallery........ 32
A Harbourside Stroll 50
Mt Eden 60
Auckland Museum............ 70
One Tree Hill 80
Ponsonby Central 84
Self-Drive Waiheke 98
Tamaki Drive.................... 108
Waitangi Treaty
Grounds 120

COVID-19

We have re-checked every business in this book before publication to ensure that it is still open after 2020's COVID-19 outbreak. However, the economic and social impacts of COVID-19 will continue to be felt long after the outbreak has been contained. Therefore many businesses, services and events referenced in this guide may experience ongoing restrictions. Some businesses may be temporarily closed, or have changed their opening hours and services; some unfortunately could have closed permanently. We suggest you check with venues before visiting for the latest information.

Welcome to Auckland & the Bay of Islands

Rugged west-coast surf beaches and myriad Hauraki Gulf islands mean the water's never far away in New Zealand's biggest city. Harbour-front restaurants frame the edge of Auckland's exciting high-rise heart, while historic and cosmopolitan inner suburbs crouch beneath a cityscape studded with volcanic cones. To the north, the Bay of Islands combines Māori and colonial history with spectacular coastal scenery.

Lion Rock, Piha, West Auckland (p111)

Top Sights

Auckland Museum
Superb Māori and Pacific Island exhibits. **p70**

Waitangi Treaty Grounds

New Zealand's most significant historic site. **p120**

Auckland Art Gallery

Showcasing both historic and contemporary NZ art. **p32**

Mt Eden

Brilliant city and harbour views from Auckland's highest volcanic cone. **p60**

West Auckland

Rugged surf beaches, forest landscapes and vineyards. **p110**

Ponsonby Central

Destination dining with food from around the world. **p84**

Tamaki Drive

Safe swimming beaches, island views and good cafes. **p108**

One Tree Hill

Soaring volcanic cone crowning Cornwall Park. **p80**

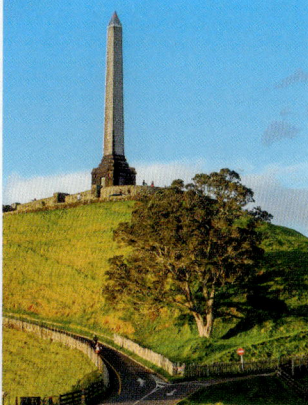

Great Barrier Island

Off-the-grid dark-sky viewing and surprising beaches. **p104**

Eating

From fine dining and authentic ethnic eateries to Waiheke Island's vineyard restaurants, Auckland offers some of New Zealand's best food. Ponsonby and Mt Eden have traditionally been dining hotspots, and Karangahape Rd and Britomart are becoming increasingly popular. For harbourside dining head to Wynyard Quarter.

BRETT ATKINSON/LONELY PLANET ©

A Diverse Dining Scene

Places to eat in Auckland are both diverse and flexible and there is often overlap between cafes, restaurants, pubs and bars. It's not uncommon for a daytime cafe serving relaxed brunches to morph into an energetic bistro serving beer and wine at night. A recent trend, especially along Karangahape Rd, is specialist wine and craft-beer bars also serving interesting and innovative food.

Global Influences

As the country's main gateway to the world, Auckland is the most diverse and cosmopolitan city in NZ. International influences abound on menus, especially the flavours of neighbouring countries in Asia. Head to Dominion Rd in Balmoral for authentic regional Chinese cuisine, or to Sandringham for Indian and Sri Lankan food. Although Auckland has the biggest population of any city in the South Pacific and is home to many families with Samoan, Cook Islands and Tongan ancestry, traditional Polynesian food isn't widely available. The best option is to attend Auckland's annual Pasifika Festival (p40), celebrating cultural performances and food and craft stalls.

Best Fine Dining

Grove Elegant central-city dining room. (p39)

Pasture Auckland's most innovative and surprising fine dining. (p75)

French Cafe One of the city's best for three decades. (p64)

Sidart Auckland's most creative degustation menus. (p88)

Fort Greene Superb sourdough sandwiches and good coffee. (p90)

Han Innovative Korean dining with good-value lunch specials of street-food classics. (p76)

Best Cafes

Scarecrow Also sells local artisan food products. (p40)

Williams Eatery Relaxed excellence from breakfast to dinner. (p54)

Winona Forever Just maybe Auckland's best counter food. (p76)

Bestie Bohemian vibe in St Kevins Arcade. (p90)

Best International

Hello Beasty Modern fusion of Japanese, Korean and Chinese flavours. (p54)

Gerome Contemporary Greek cuisine in leafy Parnell. (p75)

Gemmayze St Lebanese flavours in heritage surroundings on Karangahape Rd. (p88)

Best on a Budget

Ponsonby Central Well-priced global snacks and meals. (p84)

Foodie Websites

Check out what's new in Auckland.

- Metro (www.noted.co.nz)
- The Denizen (www.thedeinizen.co.nz)
- Cheap Eats (www.cheapeats.co.nz)

Drinking & Nightlife

From well-mixed cocktails to craft beer and NZ wines, Aucklanders like to socialise over a drink, and the city is a vibrant competitor with Wellington for having NZ's most interesting bar scene. Viaduct Harbour and Ponsonby are popular places for nightlife, but Karangahape Rd and the central city have seen new openings lately.

RABIZO/GETTY IMAGES ©

Blurring the Line

Many drinking establishments in Auckland blur the line between bar, restaurant and cafe, and a new breed of savvy bar owners is placing equal emphasis on both the drinks list and the food menu. Local provenance, sustainability and seasonality underpin the combined offerings, with natural and organic wines or one-off craft beers partnering with local seafood or foraged ingredients.

Craft Beer

Craft beer continues to grow in popularity in Auckland, and there's an increasing range of venues offering interesting and more flavourful brews. It's also becoming more prevalent on restaurant menus. Look out for beers from local Auckland brewers including Liberty, Epic, 8 Wired, Behemoth and Urbanaut. Held in late June, the annual **GABS** (Great Australasian Beer Spectapular; www.gabsfestival.com; ASB Showgrounds; late Jun) festival is a hugely enjoyable shortcut to getting to know the NZ craft-beer scene.

Best for Cocktails

Lovebucket Quirky cocktails partner with interesting sour beers. (p91)

Caretaker Cosmopolitan style with bespoke mixology. (p43)

Mo's One of Auckland's smallest (and best) cocktail bars. (p43)

Deadshot Push open the unmarked red door for a vintage vibe. (p90)

HI-SO Cocktails served with harbour views at this rooftop bar. (p43)

Best for Craft Beer

Galbraith's Alehouse Serving craft beer well before it became hip. (p66)

Garage Project Cellar Door The Auckland taproom of Wellington-based brewing innovators. (pictured above right; p66)

Vultures' Lane More than 20 taps in a convenient central-Auckland location. (p44)

Sixteen Tun Featuring lots of NZ beers in Wynyard Quarter. (p56)

Tantalus Estate Check out its Alibi Brewers Lounge on Waiheke Island. (p102)

Best for Food & Wine

Little Culprit Sophisticated snacks and a seafood raw bar. (p42)

Bar Celeste Modern bistro food and a focus on natural wines. (p91)

Madame George Hip haven with Peruvian-inspired eats. (p90)

Annabel's Channelling a Euro vibe with the best Negroni in town. (p92)

Hoppers Garden Bar Craft beer, gin cocktails and superior bar snacks. (p92)

Best for Atmosphere

Citizen Park Especially before the All Blacks are playing at nearby Eden Park. (p67)

Pineapple on Parnell A heritage gentlemen's club vibe along Parnell Rd. (p78)

Dr Rudi's Brilliant views of Viaduct Harbour. (p56)

Neck of the Woods Versatile live-music venue boosting Karangahape Rd's boho vibe. (p94)

Shopping

As NZ's biggest city, Auckland offers a wide range of shopping. Explore the city centre's arcades and laneways for more local stores beyond the international luxury brands, and take the time to discover the quirkier and more idiosyncratic shopping scenes in centrally located areas like Kingsland and Mt Eden.

Where to Shop

Followers of fashion should head to the Britomart precinct, Newmarket's Osborne St, and Ponsonby Rd. For vintage clothing, try Karangahape Rd (K Rd). Parnell offers art galleries, while the central city has excellent stores showcasing local music and writing. In the Bay of Islands both Russell and Paihia have interesting art and design stores.

What to Buy

Beyond the city's malls, the best shopping in Auckland focuses on the work of local artists and designers. Māori, Pasifika and Kiwiana designs are regularly incorporated into gifts, accessories and homewares, and repurposing material like timber and fabrics is also a popular trend. Purchase local books and music to help understand modern NZ.

Best for Fashion

Karen Walker New Zealand's best-known designer. (p95)

Kate Sylvester Playful design infusing fashion and homewares. (p79)

Huffer At home on the street or on the slopes. (p79)

Zambesi Longstanding NZ fashion icons. (p95)

Best for Books & Music

Unity Books A great independent store with good NZ selection. (p47)

Time Out An erudite highlight of Mt Eden village. (p67)

Real Groovy A huge new and pre-loved selection of vinyl. (p47)

Flying Out A fantastic selection of indie NZ sounds. (p95)

Best for Gifts & Souvenirs

Pauanesia Homewares and accessories infused with Kiwiana style. (p47)

Kura Gallery Ceramics, jewellery, design and wood carving, largely from Māori artists. (p57)

Creative & Brave Quirky and interesting design from NZ artists. (p79)

Royal Jewellery Studio Includes Māori designs featuring authentic *pounamu* (greenstone; p67).

Flying Fish Quirky and uniquely Kiwi jewellery, gifts and design. (p127)

Wood2Water Interesting design and homewares crafted from repurposed NZ timber. (p135)

Browsing Karangahape Road

Karangahape Rd has some of the city's most interesting shopping, from vintage apparel, art and design to crafts, foodstuffs, sustainable goods and homewares from local producers.

Beaches

Spanning an isthmus between two harbours, Auckland is a city blessed with fine beaches. From the city centre, Tamaki Drive ventures eastwards to Mission Bay and St Heliers, while the Hauraki Gulf islands hold surprises. West Auckland offers surf-spots, and there are excellent beaches near the Bay of Islands' towns.

BECAUZ GAO/SHUTTERSTOCK ©

Best Around Town

Mission Bay Cafes, restaurants and a heritage art-deco fountain.

St Heliers The eastern end of Tamaki Drive (p108) and easily reached on public transport.

Best of the West

Piha Wild and often windswept with the majesty of Lion Rock. (p111)

Muriwai Arcing surf beach and the avian attractions of the Takapu Refuge gannet colony. (pictured above; p111)

Best Island Escapes

Onetangi Waiheke's (p97) longest beach and also good eating and drinking.

Man O' War Bay Sheltered and scenic with a good vineyard (p101).

Medlands The most popular beach on Great Barrier Island. (p106)

West Coast Escape

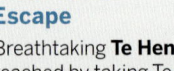

Breathtaking **Te Henga** (Bethells Beach) is reached by taking Te Henga Rd at the northern end of Scenic Dr in Auckland's western suburbs. It's a raw, black-sand beach with surf, windswept dunes and walks, such as the popular one over giant sand dunes to Lake Wainamu (starting near the bridge on the approach to the beach).

Best of the Bay of Islands

Oke Bay Definitely worth the 30km drive to get there. (p131)

Long Beach A safe family-friendly beach over the hill from Russell. (p131)

Māori Culture

Opportunities to experience Māori culture and history in Auckland and the Bay of Islands include musical performances, Māori art and design, and the flavours of a hāngi (traditional Māori earth oven). Northern historical sites date back to the 19th century, and Waiheke Island can also be explored from a Māori point of view.

UWE MOSER/GETTY IMAGES ©

Best Modern Experiences

Kura Gallery Art, crafts and design from Māori artists from around NZ. (p57)

Royal Jewellery Studio Contemporary jewellery using Māori designs and *pounamu* (greenstone). (p67)

Best Museums & Galleries

Auckland Museum Excellent Māori exhibitions and cultural performances. (p70)

Auckland Art Gallery Charles Goldie's iconic 19th-century portraits of tattooed Māori subjects. (p32)

Whare Waka Cafe Cultural performances and *hāngi* dinners at the Waitangi Treaty Grounds. (p125)

Best for Māori History

Flagstaff Hill (Maiki) Where Hōne Heke felled the British flagpole four times. (p131)

Kororipo Pā Historical walk to the former site of a Māori *pā* (fortress; p139).)

Best Tours

Potiki Adventures Waiheke Island tours from a Māori cultural perspective. (p101)

Tāmaki Hikoi Māori cultural tours around Auckland. (p37)

Visiting Marae

Visitors are welcomed onto *marae* with a customary *pōwhiri* (greeting). When meeting your host, sharing a traditional *hongi* involves gently pressing your foreheads and noses together and shaking hands.

For Kids

There are plenty of fun, active and engaging ways to keep kids fed, entertained and educated during a stay in Auckland and the Bay of Islands. Take to the water in a sailing ship or on a jetboat, challenge gravity on the Sky Tower, or learn about NZ's southern-hemisphere skies and unique birdlife.

Best Outdoor Activities

EcoZip Adventures Exciting zip lining on Waiheke Island. (p101)

Sky Tower Sky-high thrills at the top of Auckland's highest structure. (pictured above; p38)

Auckland Adventure Jet High-energy boat rides around the harbour. (p38)

Coastal Kayakers Guided tours and kayak rentals. (p123)

R Tucker Thompson Bay of Islands sailing adventures on a magnificent tall ship. (p123)

Aroha Island Self-guided walks for after-dark kiwi spotting. (p142)

Explore NZ Bay of Islands boat trips to the spectacular Hole in the Rock. (p123)

Best Indoor Activities

Stardome Stargazing, planetarium shows and a daytime children's playground. (p81)

New Zealand Maritime Museum Explore NZ's seafaring history and take a harbour cruise on a vintage yacht. (p53)

Auckland Museum Check out the Weird & Wonderful Discovery Centre. (p70)

Kelly Tarlton's Sea Life Aquarium Sharks, stingrays and penguins feature in this innovative walk-through aquarium. (p109)

Best Edible Treats

Giapo Just maybe the planet's most creative ice cream. (p39)

Island Gelato Seasonal and organic flavours on Waiheke Island. (p102)

Dragonfired Wood-fired pizza from a beachfront food caravan. (p102)

Auckland Fish Market Lots of dining options – even for fussy eaters. (p55)

Volcanoes

Auckland's volcanic field stretches right across the city and includes extinct cones, some of which are now lakes. Most surviving cones show evidence of terracing from when they formed a formidable series of Māori pā (fortified villages), and support is growing to classify the field as a Unesco World Heritage site.

Auckland's Volcanic Field

Some cities think they're tough just by living in the shadow of a volcano. Auckland is built on 50 of them and they're not all extinct. The last one to erupt was Rangitoto about 600 years ago and no one can predict when the next eruption will occur. Auckland's quite literally a hotspot – with a reservoir of magma 100km below, waiting to bubble to the surface. But relax: this has only happened 19 times in the last 20,000 years.

The most interesting volcanoes to explore are Mt Eden, One Tree Hill, North Head near Devonport, and Rangitoto (pictured above), but Mt Victoria, Mt Wellington (Maungarei), Mt Albert (Owairaka), Mt Roskill (Puketāpapa) and Lake Pupuke are all also worth a visit.

Best Ways to Experience Volcanoes

One Tree Hill Combine a walk up One Tree Hill with a morning or afternoon tackling the Coast to Coast Walkway from Onehunga to Viaduct Harbour. Visit from August to October and Cornwall Park's pastures will be full of lambs. Spring daffodils usually enliven the park's avenues from around July or August. (p80)

Mt Eden This summit is a lso part of the Coast to Coast Walkway – maybe pack a lunch and plan on a day-long adventure – and the city- and harbour-encompassing views from the top are spectacular. (p60)

Tamaki Drive There are excellent views of Rangitoto Island from the beaches lining this popular oceanfront esplanade. Book with Fergs Kayaks in Okahu Bay to embark on a kayaking trip to the city's youngest volcano. (p108)

History

Though Auckland is a young city in global terms, there are excellent opportunities to learn about the nation's history. New Zealand's wartime sacrifices are remembered at Auckland Museum, while the Bay of Islands combines Māori and colonial-missionary history. Heritage buildings include unique examples of 20th-century architecture.

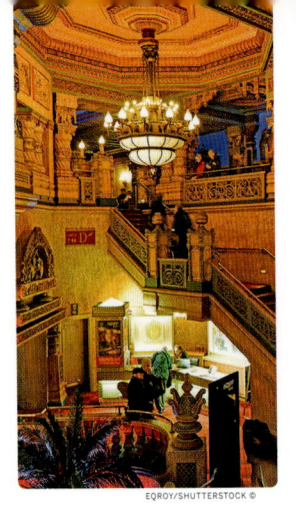

EQROY/SHUTTERSTOCK ©

Best Museums

Auckland Museum Neoclassical grandeur atop the Domain with excellent displays of NZ's military history. (p70)

New Zealand Maritime Museum Tells NZ's exciting maritime history from the Māori voyaging canoes to winning and defending yachting's America's Cup. (p53)

Te Kōngahu Museum of Waitangi Excellent showcase of the importance of modern NZ's founding document, 1840's Treaty of Waitangi. (p120)

Best Historic Buildings

St Mary's Church Admire the burnished interior and stained-glass windows of this Gothic Revival church. (p74)

St Patrick's Cathedral Dating from 1907, this Catholic church is one of Auckland's loveliest buildings. (p36)

Civic Theatre Lavish Moorish architecture decorates this 1920s theatre from cinema's golden age. (pictured; above; p36)

University Clock Tower A stellar blend of art nouveau and the Chicago School. (p37)

Best of Northland's Missionary Heritage

Pompallier Mission One of the French Catholic mission's last remaining buildings in the western Pacific. (p131)

Williams House & Gardens Historic buildings and gardens at Paihia's First Mission Station. (p124)

Kerikeri Mission Station A waterfront includes the Stone Store, NZ's oldest stone building. (p139)

Activities

Adrenaline-fuelled fun on two of Auckland's iconic landmarks proves the city can hold its own when it comes to adventure pursuits, and there's a green and sustainable tinge to activities on the city's islands. Māori culture and Auckland's great food scene are excellent reasons to book a guided tour.

Best Urban Adventures

SkyWalk Walk around the 192m-high Sky Tower. (p38)

SkyJump Take a leap of faith from the Sky Tower. (p38)

Auckland Bridge Climb & Bungy Adventure and thrills atop Auckland's famous landmark. (p37)

Auckland Adventure Jet Half an hour of harbour excitement. (p38)

Best Tours

Big Foody Food Tour Look forward to lots of gourmet tastings. (p37)

Bush & Beach The best of Auckland's spectacular West Coast. (p111)

Tamaki Hikoi Led by members of Auckland's Ngāti Whatua *iwi* (tribe). (p37)

Best Island Activities

Motubikes Ecofriendly e-bikes on Great Barrier Island. (p106)

Good Heavens Stargazing on an island Dark Sky Sanctuary. (p106)

Star Treks Excellent walking adventures on Great Barrier Island. (p105)

EcoZip Adventures Zip line above a Waiheke Island vineyard. (p101)

Best Bay of Islands Activities

R Tucker Thompson Sailing on a heritage tall ship. (p123)

Taiamai Tours Heritage Journeys Helping to paddle a traditional 12m carved Māori *waka* (war canoe; p123).

Fullers Great Sights Cruises to the Hole in the Rock and Urupukapuka Island. (p123)

Four Perfect Days

Day 1

Spend your first day exploring the highlights of the central city, beginning with breakfast at **Scarecrow** (p40), before making the short stroll along Kitchener St to the **Auckland Art Gallery** (p32).

After conquering the heights of the view-friendly **Sky Tower** (p38), head downtown for lunch at **Amano** (p39). From there, it's a short stroll either for world-beating ice cream at **Giapo** (pictured; p39), or to combine harbour views and public art at the **Lighthouse** (p36).

Cocktails at **Little Culprit** (p42) followed by innovative Indian cuisine at **Cassia** (p38) top off a great first day in NZ's biggest city.

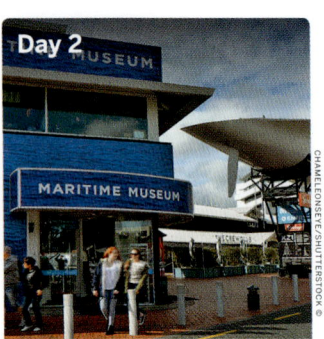

Day 2

Learn about Auckland's salty, seagoing heritage at the **New Zealand Maritime Museum** (pictured; p53), maybe going on a harbour cruise, or helping to sail a real America's Cup yacht with **Explore** (p53).

At the nearby Wynyard Quarter, enjoy the Pacific-infused menu for a harbourside lunch at **Good Luck Coconut** (p55), before catching the CityLink bus up the hill to bohemian Karangahape Rd. Interesting shopping opportunities include **Flying Out** (p95), **Crushes** (p94) and **Cross St Market** (p94), and the galleries and street art of this area are worth a look.

Head to **Gemmayze St** (p88) for dinner before a nightcap at **Lovebucket** (p91).

Day 3

Begin with coffee and breakfast at **Billy** (p71), before crossing **Auckland Domain** (pictured; p74) via the **Wintergarden** (p74) to **Auckland Museum** (p70). Highlights include the Māori and Pacific Island exhibits; make sure to check out a Māori cultural performance.

Lunch on modern Greek cuisine at **Gerome** (p75), continue to Britomart Transport Centre to catch the TāmakiLink bus along Tamaki Dr. Stop at **Kelly Tarlton's Sea Life Aquarium** (p109) to say g'day to the Antarctic penguins before continuing to Mission Bay from where it's a pleasant half-hour (2.5km) walk around the seawall to St Heliers.

Celebrate another Auckland day with dinner at **St Heliers Bay Bistro** (p109).

Day 4

Catch the ferry from Auckland's city centre to explore Waiheke Island for the day.

Either rent a car or use the island's convenient bus service to experience the highlights. For active travellers, there's the option of walking trails or vineyard **zip lining** (p101), but for many their Waiheke visit is more sybaritic.

Perhaps a swim at Onetangi Beach, wine-tasting at **Man O' War** (p101), or fine dining at **Tantalus Estate** (pictured; p102)? If you're catching a late ferry back, maybe a twilight pizza from **Dragonfired** (p102) at Little Oneroa beach before you leave? Indecisive diners may also be tempted by the seasonal fruit flavours at **Island Gelato** (p102).

Need to Know

For detailed information, see Survival Guide (p145)

Currency
New Zealand dollar (NZ$)

Language
English

Visas
Applying online in advance for an NZeTA (New Zealand Electronic Travel Authority) is mandatory for all visitors except Australian passport holders.

Money
ATMs widely available. Credit cards accepted almost universally.

Mobile Phones
Local SIM cards can be used in unlocked phones from abroad.

Time
New Zealand Standard Time (GMT/UTC plus 12 hours)

Tipping
Completely optional, but a tip of 10% is appreciated for excellent service in higher-end restaurants.

Daily Budget

Budget: Less than $175
Dorm bed: $30–40
Double room in a hostel: $90–110
Food-court meal: $15–20

Midrange: $175–500
Double room in a reasonably priced motel: $150–200
Cafe meal: $35–45

Top End: More than $500
Double room in a luxury hotel or B&B: from $300
Meal at a top restaurant: $100

Advance Planning

Three months before Organise your NZeTA and book accommodation.

One month before Book a rental car if you're travelling north to the Bay of Islands, and also secure reservations at fine-dining restaurants. Book experiences such as food and cultural tours and dark-sky viewing on Great Barrier Island.

One week before Check concerts and events on www.eventfinda.co.nz and www.aucklandnz.com/visit.

Arriving in Auckland

✈ Auckland Airport

All flights land at Auckland Airport, which has adjacent international and domestic terminals. The airport is located 21km south of the city centre. Skybus runs bright-red buses between the airport and the central city ($19). Journey time is around 60 minutes. Supershuttle is a convenient door-to-door service linking the airport to central-city hotels for $17.50 to $25 per person. Taxis from the airport take around 25 to 50 minutes and cost from $50 to $80, depending on traffic. Ride-share services Uber, Ola and Zoomy are around 30% less expensive.

Getting Around

🚍 Bus

Most convenient for visitors are the City Link, Inner Link and Outer Link services for travel in the central city and inner suburbs. Single rides cost from $1.50.

⛴ Ferry

Passenger ferries from Auckland city centre to Waiheke Island are frequent. Services also run to other Hauraki Gulf islands. Car ferries service Waiheke Island and Great Barrier Island, and Great Barrier can also be reached by plane.

🚗 Taxi

Fares are $2.60 per kilometre plus waiting time of $0.95 per minute when stationary. Ride-share apps Uber, Ola and Zoomy are available in Auckland.

Auckland Neighbourhoods

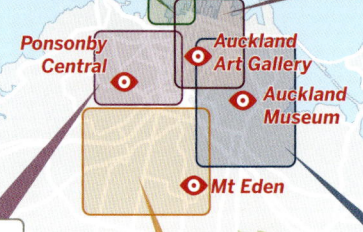

Viaduct Harbour & Wynyard Quarter (p49)
Superyachts and harbour views feature in these adjacent areas packed with popular cafes, restaurants and bars.

Ponsonby Central

Auckland Art Gallery

Auckland Museum

Mt Eden

One Tree Hill

Ponsonby & Karangahape Road (p83)
Cool Ponsonby and bohemian 'K Rd' feature some of the city's best restaurants and nightlife. There's an arty vibe with galleries, studios and street art.

Kingsland & Mt Eden (p59)
Anchored by Auckland's highest volcanic cone, this area is a popular destination for sport at Eden Park and the good cafes and restaurants of the city's leafy heritage neighbourhoods.

City Centre & Britomart (p31)
Good eating, drinking and shopping combine with the Auckland Art Gallery in the heart of the city. Embark from the Ferry Building to the islands of the Hauraki Gulf.

Tamaki Drive

Waiheke Island (p97)
Warmed by a microclimate, Waiheke's vineyards, art galleries, and excellent eating and drinking combine with active adventure and a coastline fringed with bays and beaches.

Parnell & Newmarket (p69)
Crowned by the Auckland Museum and the Domain, these central suburbs are popular for dining and shopping. Learn about New Zealand's Māori culture at the museum.

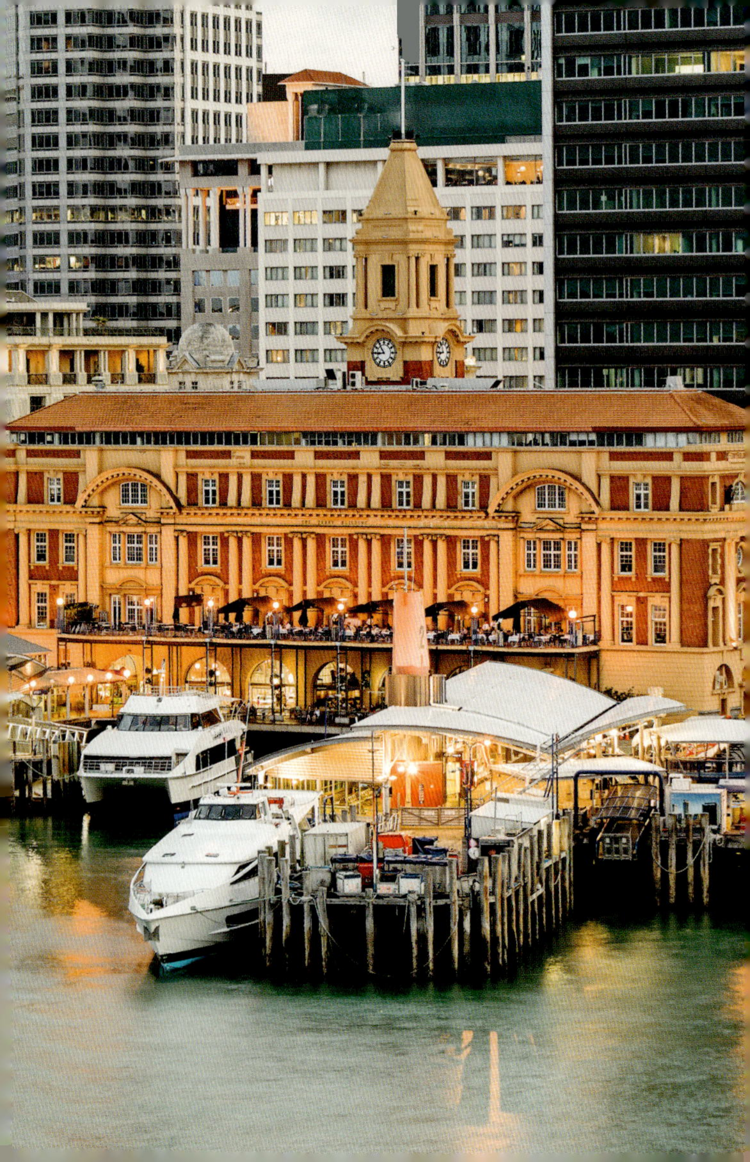

Explore
Auckland

City Centre & Britomart	31
Viaduct Harbour & Wynyard Quarter	49
Kingsland & Mt Eden	59
Parnell & Newmarket	69
Ponsonby & Karangahape Road	83
Waiheke Island	97

Top Sights

Auckland Art Gallery	32
Mt Eden	60
Auckland Museum	70
One Tree Hill	80
Ponsonby Central	84
Tamaki Drive	108

Worth a Trip

Great Barrier Island	104
West Auckland	110

Auckland's Walking & Driving Tours

A Harbourside Stroll	50
Self-Drive Waiheke	98

Ferry Building (p43) DAVID MADISON/GETTY IMAGES ©

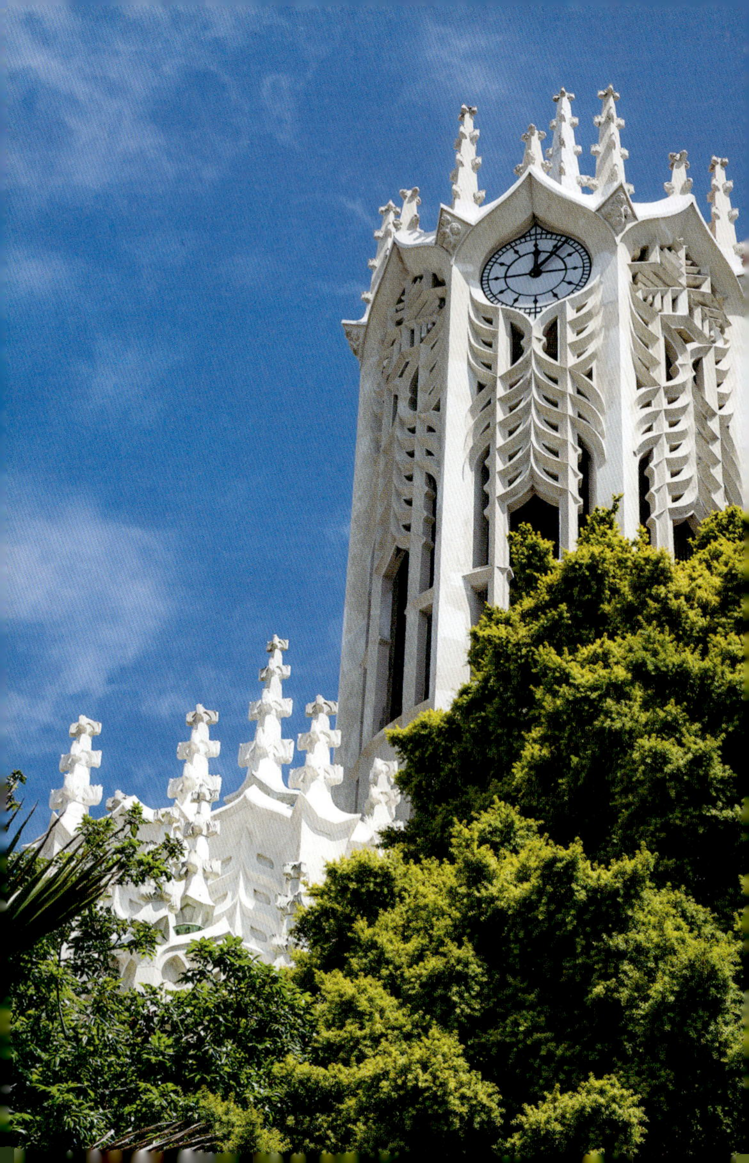

Explore
City Centre & Britomart

Framed by the harbour and Albert Park, central Auckland combines modern and heritage art, excellent cafes, restaurants and bars, and the soaring Sky Tower. The Britomart precinct showcases good shopping, eating and drinking in its repurposed historic buildings.

The Short List

- **Auckland Art Gallery (p32)** Contemplating the diverse highlights of the city's premier art gallery.

- **Lighthouse (p36)** Admiring this thought-provoking public art facing Auckland's harbour.

- **Sky Tower (p38)** Taking a leap of faith or negotiating a sky-high stroll atop Auckland's most identifiable structure.

- **Civic Theatre (p36)** Admiring the Moorish- and Indian-influenced interior of this heritage cinema.

Getting There & Around

🚌 Britomart Transport Centre is the main hub for buses arriving in central Auckland from other parts of the city. From Britomart, the InnerLink bus travels on a route taking in Parnell, Newmarket, Karangahape Rd and Ponsonby.

🚶 Auckland's city centre and Britomart area is good to explore on foot.

City Centre & Britomart Map on p34

University Clock Tower (p37), by architect RA Lippincott
DENIZUNLUSU/GETTY IMAGES ©

Top Sight
Auckland Art Gallery

Originally built in 1887 in French Renaissance style, Auckland's premier art repository is also New Zealand's most extensive and diverse collection of both national and international art. From 2008 to 2011, a striking glass-and-wood atrium was designed by FJMT and grafted onto its European frame. It's now one of the city centre's most unique buildings.

◎ MAP P34, C6

Toi o Tāmaki
☏ 09-379 1349
www.aucklandart
gallery.com
adult/student/child
$20/17/free
⏱ 10am-5pm

Showcasing the Best of New Zealand Art

Highlights of the gallery's NZ collection include the intimate 19th-century portraits of tattooed Māori subjects by Charles Goldie, and the starkly dramatic text-scrawled canvasses of Colin McCahon. Other important New Zealand art represented includes the modernist landscape and still-life paintings of Frances Hodgkins, the minimalist abstracts of Ralph Hotere, and the insightful, documentary-style photography of Marti Friedlander.

Important Overseas Artists

The gallery's impressive collection of more than 15,000 artworks also includes works by Pieter Bruegel the Younger, Guido Reni, Pablo Picasso, Paul Cézanne, Paul Gauguin and Henri Matisse.

Tours & Special Events

Free 60-minute tours depart from the foyer daily at 11.30am and 1.30pm. Check out the Events section of the gallery's website for interesting special events including music, design workshops and artists' talks. There's a cafe and an excellent shop selling many NZ-designed products. The website also hosts a comprehensive listing of other galleries and art experiences around Auckland.

★ Top Tips

o The Māori name for the gallery – Toi o Tāmaki – translates to the 'The Art of Tamaki', a reference to Tāmaki Makaurau, the Maōri name for Auckland.

o It's just a short 400m walk from the gallery through leafy Albert Park (p36) to Old Government House (p36) and the interesting University Clock Tower (p37).

✕ Take a Break

From the gallery, it's a 200m stroll to excellent coffee and lunch options at Scarecrow (p40).

For interesting Asian-inspired street food and a concise wine and craft beer list, adjourn to the Kimchi Project (p40).

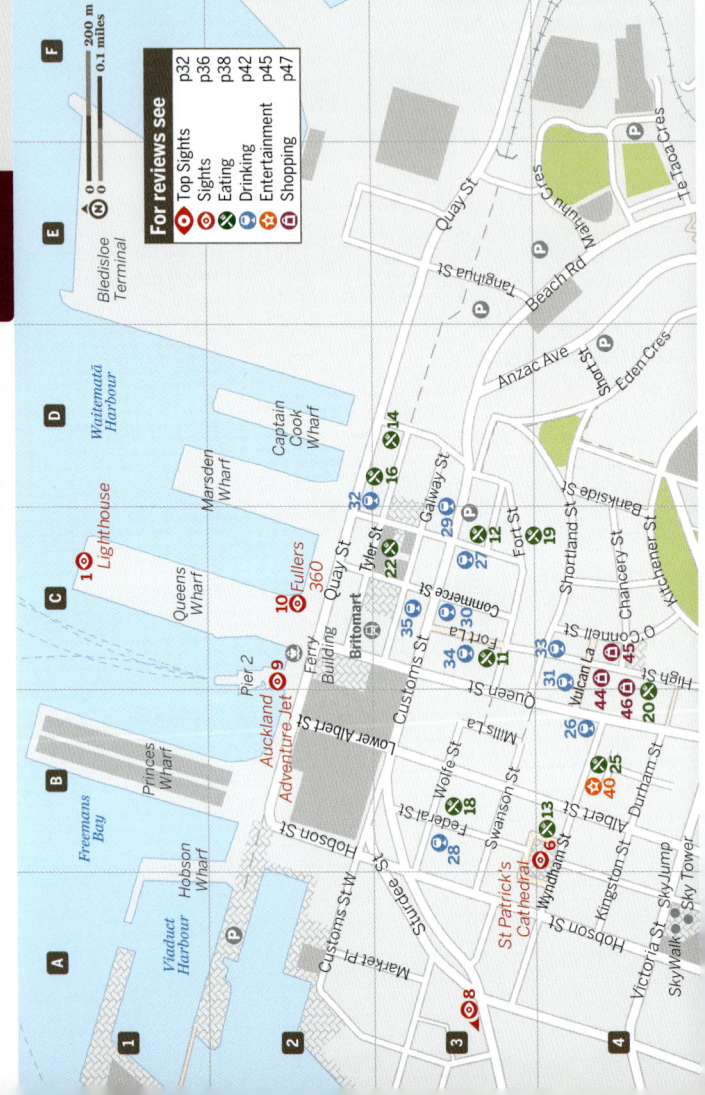

City Centre & Britomart

For reviews see
- Top Sights p32
- Sights p36
- Eating p38
- Drinking p42
- Entertainment p45
- Shopping p47

200 m / 0.1 miles

Bledisloe Terminal

Waitematā Harbour

Lighthouse

Queens Wharf

Marsden Wharf

Captain Cook Wharf

Fullers 360

Ferry Building

Britomart

Pier 2

Auckland Adventure Jet

Princes Wharf

Freemans Bay

Hobson Wharf

Viaduct Harbour

St Patrick's Cathedral

City Centre & Britomart

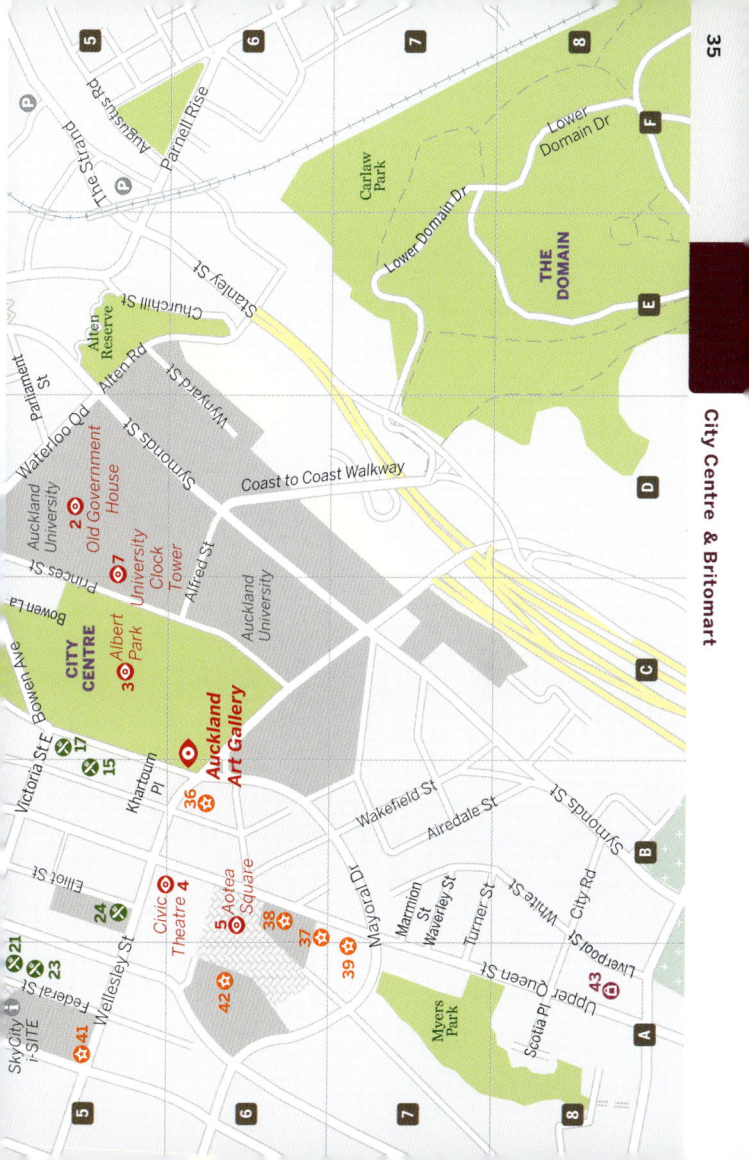

Map Labels

Streets & Areas:
- Augustus Rd
- The Strand
- Parnell Rise
- Lower Domain Dr
- Carlaw Park
- THE DOMAIN
- Stanley St
- Churchill St
- Aitken Reserve
- Aitken Rd
- Parliament St
- Waterloo Qd
- Wynyard St
- Symonds St
- Alfred St
- Princes St
- Bowen La
- Bowen Ave
- Victoria St E
- Khartoum Pl
- Wakefield St
- Airedale St
- Symonds St
- Elliott St
- Wellesley St
- Mayoral Dr
- Marmion St
- Waverley St
- Turner St
- White St
- City Rd
- Federal St
- Upper Queen St
- Scotia Pl
- Liverpool St
- Myers Park
- Coast to Coast Walkway

Numbered Points:
- 2 Old Government House
- 3 Albert Park
- 4 Civic Theatre
- 5 Aotea Square
- 7 University Clock Tower
- 36 Auckland Art Gallery
- CITY CENTRE
- Auckland University
- SkyCity i-SITE
- 15, 17, 21, 23, 24 (dining)
- 37, 38, 39, 41, 42, 43 (points of interest)

Sights

Lighthouse
PUBLIC ART

1 ◉ MAP P34, C1

Auckland's most recent installation of public art is this replica 'state house' – a form of public housing popular in NZ in the 1930s and 1940s – erected by artist Michael Parekōwhai at the end of Queens Wharf in early 2017. Maōri-influenced *tukutuku* (woven-flax) panels punctuate the exterior, while inside is a neon-lit, stainless-steel representation of British maritime explorer Captain James Cook. The house's idiosyncratic design is a commentary on sovereignty and colonialism. Best visited after dark. (Queens Wharf)

Old Government House
HISTORIC BUILDING

2 ◉ MAP P34, D5

Built in 1856, this stately building was the colony's seat of power until 1865 when Wellington became the capital. The construction is unusual in that it's actually wooden but made to look like stone. It's now used by the University of Auckland, but feel free to wander through the lush gardens. (Waterloo Quadrant; admission free)

Albert Park
PARK

3 ◉ MAP P34, C5

Hugging the hill on the city's eastern flank, Albert Park is a charming Victorian formal garden overrun by students from the neighbouring University of Auckland during term time. The park was once part of the Albert Barracks (1847), a fortification that enclosed 9 hectares during the New Zealand Wars. A portion of the original barracks wall survives at the centre of the university campus. (Princes St)

Civic Theatre
THEATRE

4 ◉ MAP P34, B5

The 'mighty Civic' (1929) is one of only seven 'atmospheric theatres' remaining in the world and a fine survivor from cinema's Golden Age. The auditorium has lavish Moorish decoration and a starlit southern-hemisphere night sky in the ceiling, complete with cloud projections and shooting stars. It's mainly used for touring musicals, international concerts and film-festival screenings. (☎09-309 2677; www.aucklandlive.co.nz/venue/the-civic)

Aotea Square
SQUARE

5 ◉ MAP P34, B6

The civic heart of the city. (Queen St)

St Patrick's Cathedral
CHURCH

6 ◉ MAP P34, B4

Auckland's Catholic cathedral (1907) is one of the city's loveliest buildings. Polished wood and Belgian stained glass lend warmth to the interior of the majestic Gothic Revival church. There's a historical display in the old confessional on the left-hand side. (☎09-303 4509; www.stpatricks.org.nz; 43 Wyndham St; ⏱7am-7pm)

University Clock Tower
ARCHITECTURE

7 ◎ MAP P34, D5

The RA Lippincott–designed Clock Tower is Auckland's architectural triumph. This stately 'ivory' tower (1926) tips its hat to art nouveau in the incorporation of NZ flora and fauna into the decoration, and the Chicago School in how it's rooted into the earth. It's usually open, so wander inside. (22 Princes St)

Auckland Bridge Climb & Bungy
ADVENTURE SPORTS

8 ◎ MAP P34, A3

Climb up or jump off the Auckland Harbour Bridge. (☏ 09-360 7748; www.bungy.co.nz; 105 Curran St; adult/child climb $130/90, bungy $165/135; ⏱ 9am-3.30pm)

Big Foody Food Tour
TOURS

Small-group city tours, including visits to markets and artisan producers and lots of tastings. Also on offer are hop-fuelled explorations of Auckland's burgeoning craft-beer scene and behind-the-scenes tours of Eden Park (p67), home of rugby and cricket in Auckland. (☏ 021 481 177, 0800 366 386; www.thebigfoody.com; per person $85-185)

Tāmaki Hikoi
CULTURAL

Guides from the Ngāti Whatua *iwi* (tribe) lead various Māori cultural tours, including walking and interpretation of sites such as Mt Eden (p60) and the Auckland Domain (p74). (☏ 021 146 9593; www.tamaki-hikoi.co.nz; 1/3hr $55/99)

Sky Tower (p38), designed by Moller Architects

Sky-High Thrills

Auckland's impossible-to-miss **Sky Tower** (Map p34, A4; 09-363 6000; www.skycityauckland.co.nz; adult/child $32/13; 8.30am-10.30pm Sun-Thu, to 11.30pm Fri & Sat Nov-Apr, 9am-10pm May-Oct), designed by Moller Architects, looks like a giant hypodermic giving a fix to the heavens. Spectacular lighting renders it space age at night and the colours change for special events. At 328m it is the southern hemisphere's tallest structure. A lift takes you up to the observation decks in 40 stomach-lurching seconds; look down through the glass floor panels if you're after an extra kick. For even more excitement, optional Sky Tower adventures include the **SkyJump** (Map p34, A4; 0800 759 925; www.skyjump.co.nz; Sky Tower; adult/child $225/175; 10am-5.15pm), a thrilling 11-second, 85km/h base wire leap from the observation deck that's more like a parachute jump than a bungy. The **SkyWalk** (Map p34, A4; 0800 759 925; www.skywalk.co.nz; Sky Tower; adult/child $150/120; 10am-4.30pm) involves circling the 192m-high, 1.2m-wide outside halo of the tower without rails or a balcony. Don't worry, it's not completely crazy – there is a safety harness.

Auckland Adventure Jet
BOATING

9 MAP P34, C2

Exciting 30-minute blasts around Auckland Harbour. (0800 255 538; www.aucklandadventurejet.co.nz; Pier 3A, Quay St; adult/child $98/58; 8am-5pm)

Fullers 360
CRUISE

10 MAP P34, C2

Offers ferries to Devonport and Waiheke, harbour cruises, and day trips to other islands in the Hauraki Gulf, including Rangitoto, Motutapu, Tiritiri Matangi and Rotoroa. (09-367 9111; www.fullers.co.nz; 6am-11pm)

Eating

Cassia
INDIAN $$$

11 MAP P34, C3

Occupying a moodily lit basement, Cassia serves modern Indian food with punch and panache. Start with a *pani puri,* a bite-sized crispy shell bursting with flavour, before devouring a decadently rich curry. The Delhi duck is excellent, as is the Goan-style snapper. Artisan gins and NZ craft beer are other highlights. Cassia is often judged Auckland's best restaurant. (09-379 9702; www.cassiarestaurant.co.nz; 5 Fort Lane; mains $30-39; noon-3pm Wed-Fri, 5.30pm-late Tue-Sat)

Depot
MODERN NZ $$

TV chef Al Brown's popular eatery (see 21 Map p34, A5) offers first-rate comfort food in informal surrounds (communal tables, butcher tiles and a constant buzz). Dishes are designed to be shared, and a pair of clever shuckers serve the city's freshest clams and oysters. It doesn't take bookings, so get there early or expect to wait. (09-363 7048; www.eatatdepot.co.nz; 86 Federal St; dishes $18-39; 7am-late)

Giapo
ICE CREAM $$

12 MAP P34, C3

That there are queues outside this boutique ice-cream shop even in the middle of winter says a lot about the magical confections that it conjures up. Expect elaborate constructions of ice-cream art topped with all manner of goodies, as Giapo's extreme culinary creativity and experimentation combines with the science of gastronomy to produce quite possibly the planet's best ice-cream extravaganzas. (09-550 3677; www.giapo.com; 12 Gore St; ice cream $12-24; 1-10pm Mon-Fri, noon to 11pm Sat & Sun;)

Grove
MODERN NZ $$$

13 MAP P34, B4

Romantic fine dining: the room is moodily lit, the menu encourages sensual experimentation and the service is effortless. If you can't find anything to break the ice from the extensive wine list, then give it up – it's never going to happen. (09-368 4129; www.thegroverestaurant.co.nz; St Patrick's Sq, Wyndham St; 4/6-course degustation $119/165; noon-3pm Thu & Fri, 6pm-late Mon-Sat)

Amano
ITALIAN $$

14 MAP P34, D3

Rustic Italian influences underpin this bistro-bakery in a repurposed warehouse in Auckland's Britomart precinct, but there's real culinary savvy evident in the open kitchen. Many dishes harness seasonal produce and ingredients from the owners' farm in West Auckland, and Amano effortlessly transitions from a buzzy caffeine-fuelled daytime cafe to a sophisticated evening bistro featuring NZ wines and craft beers. (09-394 1416; www.amano.nz; 66-68 Tyler St; mains $22-35; restaurant 7am-late, bakery 7am-4pm Mon-Sat, to 4pm Sun)

Masu
JAPANESE $$$

Part of the SkyCity complex, Masu (see 23 Map p34, A5) offers superb Japanese food – especially from the sushi bar and the robata grill – and the added attraction of refreshing cocktails made from *shochu* (Japanese liquor). (09-363 6278; www.masu.co.nz; 90 Federal St; dishes $7-46, set lunch & dinner $88-140; noon-3pm & 5.30pm-late)

Central-City Festivals

Auckland is NZ"s most cosmopolitan and diverse city, and annual cultural festivals are always a big hit. February's **Lantern Festival** (www.aucklandnz.com/lantern-festival; ☾Feb) is three days of Asian food, culture and elaborately constructed lantern tableaux in Albert Park (p36), while the city's Indian and Sri Lankan communities celebrate with music, dance and food at October's annual **Diwali Festival of Lights** (www.aucklandnz.com/diwali; ☾mid-Oct) in Aotea Square (p36). In March, Western Springs park (around 5km southwest of central Auckland) hosts the annual **Pasifika Festival** (www.aucklandnz.com/pasifika; ☾Mar), a giant Polynesian party with cultural performances and food and craft stalls.

Kimchi Project KOREAN $$

15 MAP P34, B5

Begin with a brunch of matcha latte and yuzu muesli, or escape to the palm-fringed courtyard for Asian-inspired street food, including spicy pulled-pork tacos, and bao (steamed buns) crammed with prawns. Packed with pork belly and topped with an egg, the kimchi fried rice is simple but brilliant. (☏09-302 4002; www.facebook.com/pg/thekimchiprojectnz; 20 Lorne St; snacks $12-18, mains $18-39; ☾7am-11pm Sun-Thu, 8am-midnight Fri & Sat)

Ebisu JAPANESE $$$

16 MAP P34, D3

Ebisu specialises in izakaya, a style of drinking and eating that eschews Japanese formality, yet doesn't involve food being flung around the room or chugging along on a conveyor belt. This large bar gets it exactly right, serving exquisite plates designed to be shared. Look forward to Auckland's best selection of sake, including many rare and interesting varieties. (☏09-300 5271; www.ebisu.co.nz; 116-118 Quay St; large plates $34-42; ☾noon-3pm Mon-Fri, 5.30pm-late daily)

Scarecrow CAFE $$

17 MAP P34, C5

Organic and vegan ingredients shine at this bustling cafe near Albert Park. Bentwood chairs add a Gallic ambience, and the menu veers towards European and Middle Eastern flavours. Try the *shakshuka* baked eggs or house-smoked fish cakes for brunch. A compact deli section sells local artisan food products, and there's also an on-site florist. (☏09-377 1333; www.scarecrow.co.nz; 33 Victoria St East; mains $16-28; ☾7am-5pm Mon-Fri, 8am-5pm Sat & Sun, kitchen closes 3pm; ☝)

Federal & Wolfe CAFE $$

18 MAP P34, B3

Packing crates and mismatched chairs lend an air of recycled chic to this corner cafe. Look forward to first-rate coffee and delicious food, much of it organic and free-range. (📞09-359 9113; www.facebook.com/FederalandWolfeCafe; 10 Federal St; mains $15-22; ⏰7am-3pm Mon-Fri, 8am-2pm Sat)

O'Connell Street Bistro
EUROPEAN $$$

O'Connell Street (see 33 🚇 Map p34, C4) is a grown-up treat, with smart decor and wonderful food and wine, serving lunchtime power brokers and dinnertime daters alike. If you're dining before 7.15pm, a fixed-price menu is available. (📞09-377 1884; www.oconnellstbistro.com; 3 O'Connell St; mains $32-45, fixed menu 2/3 courses $38/48; ⏰11.30am-3pm & 5-11pm Mon-Fri, 5-11pm Sat)

Ima
MIDDLE EASTERN $$

19 ❌ MAP P34, C3

Named after the Hebrew word for mother, Ima's menu features an array of Israeli, Palestinian, Yemeni and Lebanese comfort food, along with meat pies and sandwiches at lunchtime. Rustle up a group for Ima's excellent shared dinners and feast on whole fish, chicken *mesachan* (a whole bird slow-cooked with herbs and spices and then grilled) or slow-cooked lamb shoulder. (📞09-377 5252; www.imacuisine.co.nz; 53 Fort St; breakfast & lunch $12-26, dinner shared dishes $15-30; ⏰7am-10pm Mon-Fri, from 8.30am Sat)

Chuffed
CAFE $

20 ❌ MAP P34, B4

Concealed in a lightwell at the rear of a building, this hip place, liberally coated in street art, is a definite contender for the inner-city's best cafe. Grab a seat on the terrace and tuck into cooked breakfasts, Wagyu burgers, lamb shanks or flavour-packed toasted sandwiches. There's a small but well-considered list of local beers and wines. (📞09-367 6801; www.chuffedcoffee.com; 43 High St; mains $10-21; ⏰7am-4pm Mon-Fri, from 9am Sat & Sun)

Federal Delicatessen
AMERICAN $$

21 ❌ MAP P34, A5

Celebrity chef Al Brown's take on a New York Jewish deli serves simple

Chuffed

stuff like bagels and sandwiches, matzo-ball soup and lots of delicious comfort food to share (turkey meatloaf, spit-roasted chicken, New York strip steak). White butcher tiles, vinyl booth seating and waiters in 1950s uniforms add to the illusion. (☏09-363 7184; www.thefed.co.nz; 86 Federal St; mains $11-29; ⏰7am-late)

Ortolana ITALIAN $$

22 MAP P34, C3

Mediterranean and regional Italian flavours are showcased at this stylish restaurant. Dishes are as artfully arranged as they are delicious, and much of the produce comes from the owners' small farm in rural west Auckland. Some of the sweets come from its sister patisserie, the very fabulous Milse, next door. It doesn't take bookings. (www.ortolana.co.nz; 33 Tyler St; mains $25-35; ⏰7am-11pm)

Gusto at the Grand ITALIAN $$

23 MAP P34, A5

One of the more affordable eateries in the big, brash SkyCity casino complex, Gusto excels in delivering fresh pasta dishes, all of which are made from scratch when you order. The space feels like an extension of the hotel lobby, but you can sit at the marble counter and watch the action in the kitchen. (www.skycityauckland.co.nz; SkyCity Grand Hotel, 90 Federal St; mains $22-44; ⏰noon-2.30pm & 5pm-late; 🍴)

Ela Cuisine INDIAN $$

24 MAP P34, B5

Tucked away at the rear of the Elliott Stables food court, this excellent Indian eatery serves lip-smacking curries (Kerala beef, coconut lamb shank, 'butterless' chicken etc) and *masala dosa* (stuffed pancakes), each accompanied by a generous serving of rice and salad. It's great value too. (☏09-379 2710; www.elacuisine.co.nz; 41 Elliott St; mains $15-27; ⏰11.45am-2.45pm & 5-9.30pm; 🍴)

Revive VEGETARIAN $

25 MAP P34, B4

Vegetarian heaven with an enticing salad bar and affordable daily meal deals. (☏09-303 0420; www.revive.co.nz; 24 Wyndham St; mains $12-15; ⏰9am-7pm Mon-Thu, to 4pm Fri; 🍴)

Drinking

Little Culprit COCKTAIL BAR

26 MAP P34, B4

Some of Auckland's most interesting cocktails feature at this stylish bar, and the owners' background in restaurants also shines through. Graze on a platter of cheese and charcuterie or indulge in a savoury waffle with duck-liver parfait. People-watch at pavement level or adjourn to the more intimate lower lounge downstairs. There's a good selection of natural wines too. (www.littleculprit.co.nz; cnr Wyndham & Queen Sts; ⏰noon-1am Mon-Thu, to 2am Fri & Sat)

Exploring the Hauraki Gulf

From the **Ferry Building** (Map p34, C2; 99 Quay St) in downtown Auckland, it's possible to catch boats for day trips to other islands in the Hauraki Gulf. Just 600 years old and sloping elegantly from the ocean, 259m-high **Rangitoto** (www.rangitoto.org) is the largest and youngest of Auckland's volcanic cones. Catch a **ferry** (09-367 9111; www.fullers.co.nz; adult/child return $36/18) and walk up the exposed scoria slopes to the summit – bring walking shoes, food and water – or take a ride around the island on the canopied tractor-led **'Volcanic Explorer'** (09-367 9111; www.fullers.co.nz; adult/child incl ferry $70/35; departs Auckland 9.15am & 12.15pm) road train.

Tiritiri Matangi (www.tiritirimatangi.org.nz) is a 220-hectare, predator-free island and home to the tuatara (a prehistoric lizard) and lots of endangered native birds, including the rare and colourful takahē. Other birds include the bellbird, stitchbird, saddleback, whitehead, kakariki, kokako, little spotted kiwi, brown teal, New Zealand robin, fernbird and penguins; 78 different species have been sighted in total.

Book a guided walk ($5) with your ferry ticket; the guides know where all the really cool birds hang out.

HI-SO COCKTAIL BAR

27 MAP P34, C3

Every burgeoning international city needs a good rooftop bar, and the stylish HI-SO at the So/Auckland ticks all the boxes. Futuristic decor includes a shimmering wall of neon, with the dramatic interior segueing to an outdoor terrace with island and harbour views. Signature cocktails include the chamomile-infused Gulf Spritzer, and bar snacks run from oysters to tiger prawns. (www.so-auckland.com; cnr Customs St E & Gore St; 4pm-midnight)

Mo's BAR

28 MAP P34, B3

This tiny corner bar makes you want to invent problems for the bartender to solve with soothing words and an expertly poured martini. (09-366 6066; www.mosbar.co.nz; cnr Wolfe & Federal Sts; 2pm-late Mon-Fri, from 6pm Sat;)

Caretaker COCKTAIL BAR

29 MAP P34, C3

New York style infuses this cocktail bar concealed behind an old door inscribed with the title 'Caretaker'. The decor is equally eclectic, and a handful of tables and leather sofas

> **By Ferry to Devonport**
>
> A popular excursion from central Auckland is across the harbour to the heritage suburb of Devonport. With well-preserved Victorian and Edwardian buildings, good shopping and loads of cafes, it's a pleasant place to visit. There are also two volcanic cones to climb and easy access to the first of the North Shore's beaches. Fullers 360 (p38) ferries to Devonport (adult/child return $15/7.50, 12 minutes) depart from the Ferry Building (p43) at least every 30 minutes from 6.15am to 11.30pm (until 1am Friday and Saturday), and from 7.15am to 10pm on Sunday and public holidays.

means the bar always feels intimate and convivial. Choose from the very considered cocktail list, or just describe what you like and the bartenders will work their bespoke mixology magic. (www.caretaker.net.nz; Roukai Lane; ⏰5pm-3am)

La Fuente   COCKTAIL BAR

30 MAP P34, C3

Auckland's only bar specialising in the potent Mexican spirit mezcal, La Fuente (The Fountain) is also a fine spot to partner an excellent selection of wine and craft beer with Latin American–inspired snacks, including ceviche and cheese-and-jalapeño croquettes. The knowledgeable bartenders will guide you through more than 20 different mezcals from the Mexican region of Oaxaca. (☎09-303 0238; www.lafuente.co.nz; 23 Customs St E; ⏰11am-late)

Vultures' Lane   PUB

31 MAP P34, C4

With 28 taps, more than 90 bottled beers and sports on the TV, this pleasantly grungy historic pub is popular with Auckland's savviest craft-beer fans. Check the website for what's currently on tap, and also for news of regular tap takeovers from some of NZ's best brewers. (☎09-300 7117; www.vultureslane.co.nz; 10 Vulcan Lane; ⏰11.30am-late)

The Brit   PUB

32 MAP P34, D2

A modern reimagining of a traditional British pub, this self-described 'pub and eatery' enjoys a convenient location near the Ferry Building. Some of Auckland's biggest windows and highest ceilings instill a spacious and airy ambience, and a drinks list focussed on NZ wine and craft beer partners with reworked pub classics like burgers, fish and chips, and bangers and mash. (☎09-374 3952; www.thebrit.co.nz; 122 Quay St; ⏰11am-late)

Hotel DeBrett   BAR

33 MAP P34, C4

Grab a New Zealand craft beer in the colourful Cornerbar or a cocktail in the art-deco Housebar at the very heart of this chic hotel. (www.hoteldebrett.com; 2 High St; ⏲noon-late)

Jefferson BAR

34 📍 MAP P34, C3

Lit by the golden glow of close to 600 different whisky bottles, this subterranean den is a sophisticated spot for a nightcap. There's no list – talk to the knowledgable bar staff about the kind of thing you're after (peaty, smooth, smoky, not too damaging to the wallet) and they'll suggest something. (www.thejefferson.co.nz; basement, Imperial Bldg, Fort Lane; ⏲4pm-1am Mon-Thu, to 3am Fri & Sat)

Xuxu COCKTAIL BAR

35 📍 MAP P34, C3

A winning combination of Asian-tinged cocktails and tasty dumplings. (📞09-309 5529; www.xuxu.co.nz; cnr Galway & Commerce Sts; ⏲noon-late Mon-Fri, from 5pm Sat)

Entertainment

Academy Cinemas CINEMA

36 ⭐ MAP P34, B6

Foreign and art-house films in the basement of the Central Library. Cheap $5 movies on Wednesdays. (📞09-373 2761; www.academycinemas.co.nz; 44 Lorne St; tickets adult/child $16/10)

Britomart

Q Theatre
THEATRE

37 ⭐ MAP P34, B6

Theatre by various companies and intimate live music. Silo Theatre (www.silotheatre.co.nz) often performs here. (☎09-309 9771; www.qtheatre.co.nz; 305 Queen St)

Auckland Town Hall
CLASSICAL MUSIC

38 ⭐ MAP P34, B6

This elegant Edwardian venue (1911) hosts the New Zealand Symphony Orchestra (www.nzso.co.nz) and Auckland Philharmonia (www.apo.co.nz), among others. Also used for concerts by touring international bands. (☎09-309 2677; www.aucklandlive.co.nz; 305 Queen St)

Classic Comedy Club
COMEDY

39 ⭐ MAP P34, A7

Stand-up performances most nights, with legendary late-night shows during the **Comedy Festival** (www.comedyfestival.co.nz; ⌚Apr-May), which takes place each year. (☎09-373 4321; www.comedy.co.nz; 321 Queen St; ⌚6.30pm-late)

Ding Dong Lounge
LIVE MUSIC

40 ⭐ MAP P34, B4

Rock, indie and alternative sounds from live bands and DJs, washed down with craft beer. (☎09-377 4712; www.dingdongloungenz.com; 26 Wyndham St; ⌚6pm-4am Wed-Fri, from 8pm Sat)

Auckland Town Hall

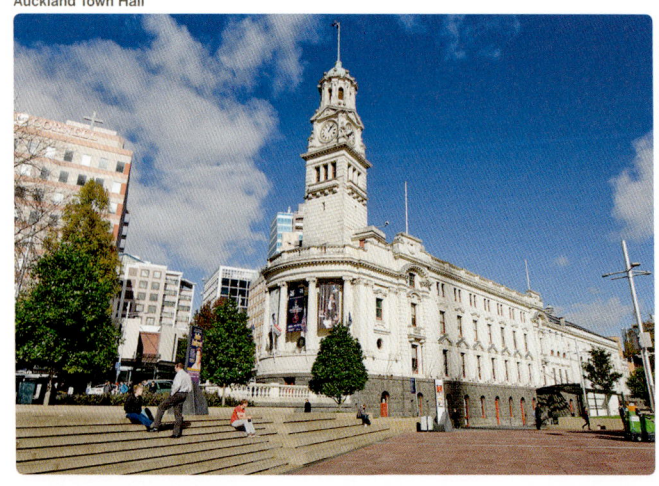

SkyCity Theatre THEATRE
41 MAP P34, A5

Theatre within the casino complex, used for musicals, comedy and the occasional concert. (☎09-363 6000; www.skycity.co.nz; cnr Wellesley & Hobson Sts)

Aotea Centre THEATRE
42 MAP P34, A6

Comprises the small Herald Theatre (drama) and the vast ASB Theatre (used for dance, ballet, opera and musicals). New Zealand Opera (www.nzopera.com) regularly performs here. (☎09-309 2677; www.aucklandlive.co.nz; 50 Mayoral Dr)

Shopping

Real Groovy MUSIC
43 MAP P34, A8

Masses of new, secondhand and rare releases in vinyl and CD format, plus concert tickets, posters, DVDs, books, magazines and clothes. (☎09-302 3940; www.realgroovy.co.nz; 520 Queen St; ⏲9am-7pm)

Unity Books BOOKS
44 MAP P34, C4

The inner city's best independent bookshop with a fine selection of NZ tomes. (☎09-307 0731; www.unitybooks.co.nz; 19 High St; ⏲8.30am-7pm Mon-Fri, 10am-6pm Sat & Sun)

Strangely Normal CLOTHING
45 MAP P34, C4

Quality, NZ-made men's tailored shirts straight out of *Blue Hawaii* sit alongside hipster hats, sharp shoes and cufflinks. (☎09-309 0600; www.strangelynormal.com; 19 O'Connell St; ⏲10am-6pm Mon-Sat, 11am-4pm Sun)

Pauanesia GIFTS & SOUVENIRS
46 MAP P34, C4

Homewares and gifts with a Polynesian and Kiwiana influence. (☎09-366 7282; www.pauanesia.co.nz; 35 High St; ⏲9.30am-6.30pm Tue-Fri, 10am-5pm Sat-Mon)

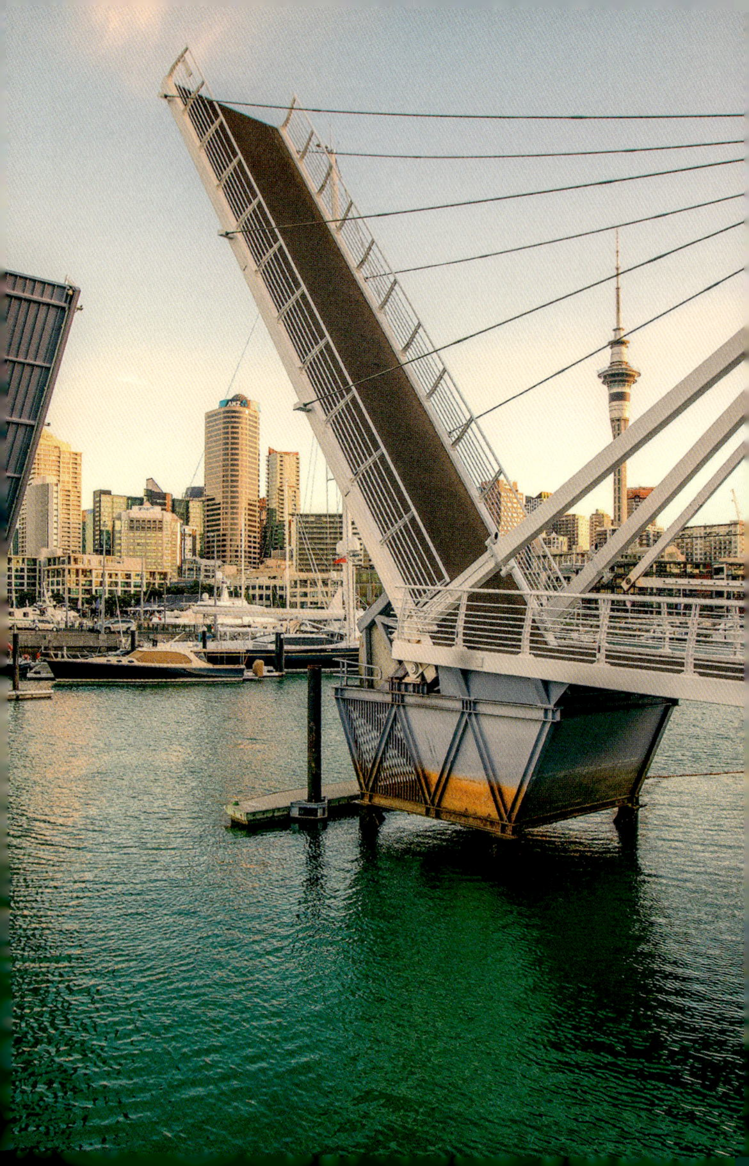

Explore
Viaduct Harbour & Wynyard Quarter

Once a busy commercial port, Viaduct Harbour was transformed for the 1999/2000 and 2003 America's Cup yachting events, and is now a popular eating and drinking precinct. Connected to Viaduct Harbour by a footbridge, Wynyard Quarter combines public plazas, waterfront bars, eateries and a children's playground.

The Short List

- **New Zealand Maritime Museum (p53)** Taking a heritage harbour cruise and learning about this island nation's seafaring history.

- **Auckland Fish Market (p55)** Combining a New Zealand wine or craft beer with fresh seafood at a diverse range of eateries.

- **Silo Park (p55)** Enjoying this area's harbourside summer-time buzz of markets, music and movies.

- **Auckland Seaplanes (p53)** Soaring above the City of Sails to a vineyard lunch on Waiheke Island.

- **Explore (p53)** Experiencing the thrill of America's Cup–style match racing on Auckland Harbour.

Getting There & Around

🚶 Viaduct Harbour and Wynyard Quarter are easily walkable from the central city.

🚌 The CityLink bus operates on a convenient route linking the Wynyard Quarter to Britomart, the city centre (Queen St) and Karangahape Rd.

Viaduct Harbour & Wynyard Quarter Map on p52

Viaduct Harbour MARIA KAZAKOVA1 /SHUTTERSTOCK ©

Walking Tour

A Harbourside Stroll

In the past, Auckland has not made the most of the city's harbour-front location, but with success in America's Cup yachting providing the catalyst for investment, the area around Viaduct Harbour and Wynyard Quarter is developing as a hub for accommodation, eating and drinking, and residential living.

Walk Facts

Start Giraffe; Quay St/ Lower Albert St, Bus Stop 1346

End Dr Rudi's; Quay St/ Lower Albert St, Bus Stop 1346

Length 2.5km; 90 minutes

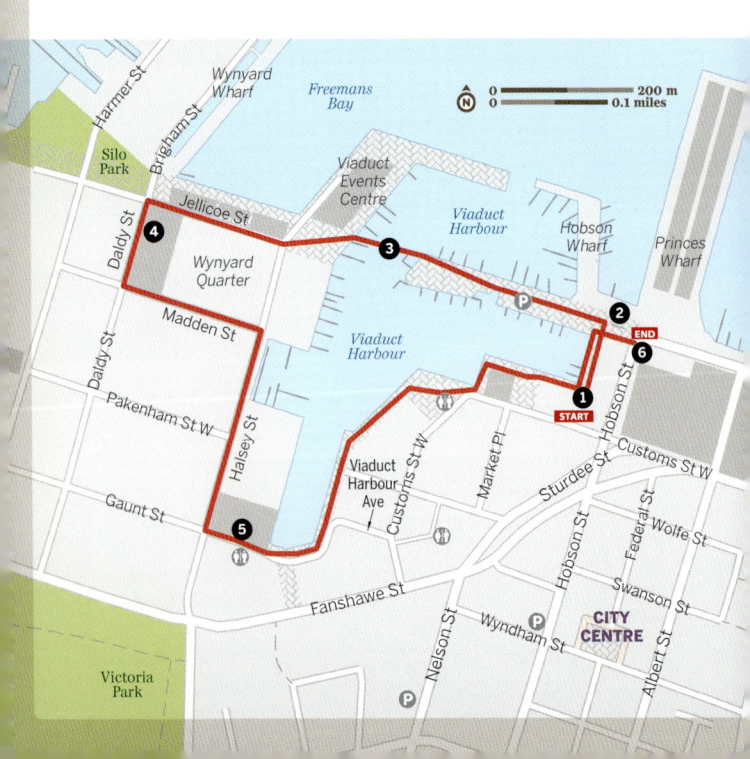

❶ Giraffe

Kick off this walk around Auckland's regenerating inner harbour amid the superyachts and sunshine of the city's Viaduct. Owned by well-known Auckland chef Simon Gault, **Giraffe** (p56) is a good spot for the first coffee of the day and has interesting ways with eggs, including a Thai-style omelette.

❷ New Zealand Maritime Museum

Stroll around the Viaduct's harbour from Giraffe to the **New Zealand Maritime Museum** (p53), stopping to secure information on an America's Cup–style yachting adventure with **Explore** (p53). The gleaming white catamaran outside the museum was NZ's challenger for the Cup in 1988.

❸ Te Wero Bridge

After learning about the City of Sails' seagoing history, cross Te Wero Bridge to Wynyard Quarter. A modern version of a bascule bridge (drawbridge), its spans rise and fall to allow boats through to the compact inner harbour. If you have to wait a little, see if anyone is tackling the **SkyWalk** (p38) on the **Sky Tower** (p38) to your left.

❹ Auckland Fish Market

Wander past North Wharf's harbourside bars and restaurants to this upscale **food court** (p55). There's also a relaxed a courtyard bar with live music on some weekend afternoons. A few of Auckland's best food trucks occasionally drop by.

❺ Sofitel Auckland Viaduct Harbour

From the Auckland Fish Market continue south on Daldy St – there's a good kids' playground in Daldy Street Park – before turning left down Gaunt St to the **Sofitel Auckland Viaduct Harbour** (☏09-909 9000; www.sofitel-auckland.com; 21 Viaduct Harbour Ave; d from $449; P 🛜 🏊). Stop for another coffee at the hotel's harbourside cafe.

❻ Dr Rudi's

From the Sofitel, walk 750m around the pedestrian walkway lining the marina back to Viaduct Harbour. There are views across the water to the new Park Hyatt luxury hotel, one of the big developments initiated for Auckland's hosting of the America's Cup yachting event in March 2021. Toast NZ's sailing successes with a drink and fine views at **Dr Rudi's** (p56).

Viaduct Harbour & Wynyard Quarter

Princes Wharf

Princes Wharf i-SITE
DOC Auckland Visitor Centre

New Zealand Maritime Museum

Auckland Hop On, Hop Off Explorer

Freemans Bay

Hobson Wharf

Viaduct Harbour

Viaduct Harbour

Explore

CITY CENTRE

Viaduct Events Centre

Karanga Kiosk

Auckland Seaplanes

Wynyard Quarter

Silo Park
Silo Cinema & Markets

For reviews see
- Sights p53
- Eating p54
- Drinking p56
- Entertainment p57
- Shopping p57

Sights

New Zealand Maritime Museum
MUSEUM

1 ⊙ MAP P52, E3

This museum traces NZ's seafaring history, from Māori voyaging canoes to the America's Cup. Re-creations include a tilting 19th-century steerage-class cabin and a 1950s beach store and bach (holiday home). 'Blue Water Black Magic' is a tribute to Sir Peter Blake, the Whitbread Round the World and America's Cup–winning yachtsman who was murdered in 2001 on an environmental monitoring trip in the Amazon. Packages incorporating harbour cruises on heritage boats, including a ketch-rigged scow and a vintage motor launch, are also available. (☏09-373 0800; www.maritimemuseum.co.nz; Corner of Quay and Hobson Sts; adult/child $20/10, incl harbour cruise $53/27; ⊙10am-5pm, free tours 10.30am & 1pm Mon-Fri)

Auckland Seaplanes
SCENIC FLIGHTS

2 ⊙ MAP P52, C2

Flights in a cool 1960s floatplane that explore Auckland's harbour and islands. The company's location and departure point may change in the future, so check the website for the latest. (☏09-390 1121; www.aucklandseaplanes.com; 171 Halsey St; per person from $225; ⊙8am-7pm)

Explore
BOATING

3 ⊙ MAP P52, E3

Shoot the breeze for two hours on a genuine America's Cup yacht (adult/child $190/135), take a 90-minute cruise on a glamorous large yacht (adult/child $99/60) or tuck into a 2½-hour Harbour Dinner Cruise (adult/child $145/99). (☏0800 397 567; www.exploregroup.co.nz; Viaduct Harbour)

Auckland Hop On, Hop Off Explorer
BUS

4 ⊙ MAP P52, F3

Two services – the red or blue route – take in the best of the waterfront, including attractions along Tamaki Dr (p1068), or highlights including Mt Eden (p60) and

Scow owned by the NZ Maritime Museum

MICHAEL W NZ/SHUTTERSTOCK ©

Festival Frenzy

Framing the waterfront, this part of Auckland is a favourite location for various events and festivals throughout the year. In September, Auckland's 'City of Sails' nickname is reinforced with the annual **Auckland on Water Boat Show** (www.auckland-boatshow.com; Viaduct Harbour; ⊙Sep). Even if you're not in the market for anything nautical or maritime, it's good fun to take in the superyachts thronging Viaduct Harbour. A month earlier in August, **New Zealand Fashion Week** (www.nzfashionweek.com; ⊙Aug) presents the new collections of established Auckland designers, including Zambesi and Kate Sylvester, and the best of the industry's innovative new talents.

the **Auckland Zoo** (☎09-360 3805; www.aucklandzoo.co.nz; Motions Rd; adult/child $24/13; ⊙9.30am-5pm, last entry 4.15pm). Red-route buses depart from near Princes Wharf hourly from 10am to 3pm (more frequently in summer), and it's possible to link to the blue route at the Auckland Museum (p70). Two-day passes are also available, and both passes include ferry tickets for Devonport. (☎0800 439 756; www.explorerbus.co.nz; adult/child per day $45/20, 2 days $55/25)

Eating

Hello Beasty   ASIAN $$

5 ✕ MAP P52, E3

Japanese, Korean and Chinese flavours are all filtered through a fun contemporary vibe near Auckland's Viaduct Harbour. Secure a spot with ocean views, and fill your table with shared plates, including steamed bao buns, smoky Japanese-style *tsukune* sausage and barbecued eggplant. The concise drinks list includes sake cocktails and spritzes, and NZ lamb and seafood are regularly featured. (☎021 554 496; https://hellobeasty.nz; 95-97 Customs St W; shared plates $12-38; ⊙11am-11pm; ✈)

Williams Eatery   CAFE $$

6 ✕ MAP P52, B3

Serving the residential precinct emerging around the Wynyard Quarter, Williams Eatery's always-excellent coffee partners with hotcakes and mandarin curd for brunch, while the dinner menu includes lamb and seafood specials and brillian pasta. On-trend organic and natural wines, classic Mimosa and Negroni cocktails, and regional Auckland craft beers all help to pleasantly blur the line between lunch and dinner. (☎09-373 3906; www.williamseatery.co.nz; 85 Daldy St; mains $15-33; ⊙7am-3pm Mon-Wed, to late Thu & Fri, 8am-late Sat, 8am-4pm Sun)

Baduzzi

ITALIAN $$

7 MAP P52, B2

This smart and sassy eatery does sophisticated spins on meatballs – try the crayfish ones – and other robust but elegant Italian dishes. Cosy up in the intimate booths, grab a seat at the bar or soak up some Auckland sunshine outside. (09-309 9339; www.baduzzi.co.nz; cnr Jellicoe St & Fish Lane; mains $23-38; 11.30am-late;)

Saint Alice

BISTRO $$

8 MAP P52, E3

Viaduct Harbour views and a subtle maritime design vibe make Saint Alice one of Auckland's best places to soak up the harbour-city ambience. Both bar and bistro, it's a bustling place, and standouts on the seasonal menu always include wood-roasted lamb and the restaurant's signature dish of oyster McMuffins with black garlic aioli. (www.saintalice.co.nz; Level 1, 204 Quay St; shared plates $14-39; 11.30am-late)

Good Luck Coconut

ASIAN $$

9 MAP P52, B2

Good Luck Coconut's blending of Pacific and Asian design and flavours really suits the overall vibe of the city, especially when combined with briny harbour views in the Wynyard Quarter. Shared plates include *ika mata (*raw fish cured in coconut and lime), crab sliders and a great pork *katsu* burger with kimchi. Great Pacific-inspired cocktails too. (09-303 0440; www.thegoodluckcoconut.co.nz; 39 Jellicoe St; shared plates $14-23; noon-late Thu-Sun, from 4.30pm Wed)

Auckland Fish Market

MARKET $$

10 MAP P52, B2

A makeover in early 2019 incorporated a seafood-focused upscale food court and a relaxed courtyard bar with a good beer and wine selection. Dining options include sashimi, Thai food, South American barbecue, pizza, and fish and chips. Check online for details of regular seafood cookery classes including Vietnamese and Mediterranean flavours. (09-379 1490;

Movies, Markets & Food Trucks

Located under towering silos adorned with colourful street art, the **Silo Park** (Map p52, A1; www.silopark.co.nz; Silo Park; Dec-Easter) area at the northern end of the Wynyard Quarter is a popular destination throughout summer. Classic movies are screened outdoors on Friday nights, and there are sometimes markets with food trucks, DJs and craft stalls on Friday nights and Saturday and Sunday afternoons. Look forward to excellent ocean views, especially taking in the graceful arch of the Auckland Harbour Bridge. There's also a good children's playground nearby.

www.afm.co.nz; 22-32 Jellicoe St; mains $15-25; 7am-9pm)

Giraffe
MODERN NZ $$$

11 MAP P52, E3

Giraffe combines a stylish but casual harbourside dining room with a local and seasonal menu. The restaurant was named by owner Simon Gault's then 3-year-old daughter, and the menu is packed with sophisticated and superior versions of comfort food such as lamb shanks, fish pie and roast chicken. There's also a pricey, but very impressive, selection of steaks. (09-358 1093; www.girafferestaurant.co.nz; 85-87 Customs St West; mains $28-48; 7am-late Mon-Fri, from 8am Sat & Sun)

Drinking

Sixteen Tun
CRAFT BEER

12 MAP P52, B2

The glister of burnished copper perfectly complements the liquid amber on offer here in the form of dozens of NZ craft beers by the bottle and a score on tap. If you can't decide, go for a good-value tasting 'crate' of 200mL serves. (09-368 7712; www.16tun.co.nz; 10-26 Jellicoe St; 11.30am-late)

Dr Rudi's
MICROBREWERY

13 MAP P52, F3

Viaduct Harbour's best views – usually including a bevy of visiting superyachts – combine with Dr Rudi's very own craft beers and a menu featuring wood-fired

Viaduct Harbour

How to Walk Across New Zealand

Heading right across the country from the Tasman to the Pacific (actually only 16km), the **Coast to Coast Walkway** (Map p52; www.aucklandcity.govt.nz) encompasses One Tree Hill, Mt Eden, the Domain and the university, keeping mainly to reserves rather than city streets. Linking Onehunga to Viaduct Harbour, it can be done in either direction, but our recommendation is to catch the train to Onehunga so you can celebrate with a cold beer at the Viaduct when you finish. From Onehunga station, take Onehunga Mall up to Princes St, turn left and pick up the track at the inauspicious park by the motorway. Heading north from Onehunga look for the blue track markers.

pizza and excellent seafood and barbecue platters designed to defeat even the hungriest group. There are also a couple of tenpin bowling lanes to get active on. (021 048 7946; cnr Quay & Hobson Sts; 8am-4am Mon-Fri, from 11am Sat & Sun)

Wynyard Pavilion   BAR

14 MAP P52, B2

Formerly a harbourside warehouse, Wynyard Pavilion's high-ceilinged heritage space is now one of the area's most versatile spots to eat, drink and take in maritime views. Oysters and kingfish feature from the raw bar; pizza ingredients include smoked salmon or spicy 'nduja sausage; and the watermelon and feta salad is perfect for warmer days. Try to snaffle a seat outside. (09-303 1002; www.facebook.com/wynyardpavilion; 17 Jellicoe St; 11am-11pm)

Entertainment

ASB Waterfront Theatre   THEATRE

15 MAP P52, C3

The ASB Waterfront Theatre is used by the Auckland Theatre Company and also for occasional one-off shows and concerts. A good selection of bars and restaurants are nearby. (0800 282 849; www.asbwaterfronttheatre.co.nz; 138 Halsey St)

Shopping

Kura Gallery   ARTS & CRAFTS

16 MAP P52, E4

Tucked away behind the Viaduct Harbour restaurant strip, Kura is a good place to find art, crafts and design from Māori artists. Works for sale include ceramics, jewellery and wood carving. (09-302 1151; www.kuragallery.co.nz; 95a Customs St W; 10am-6pm Mon-Fri, 11am-4pm Sat & Sun)

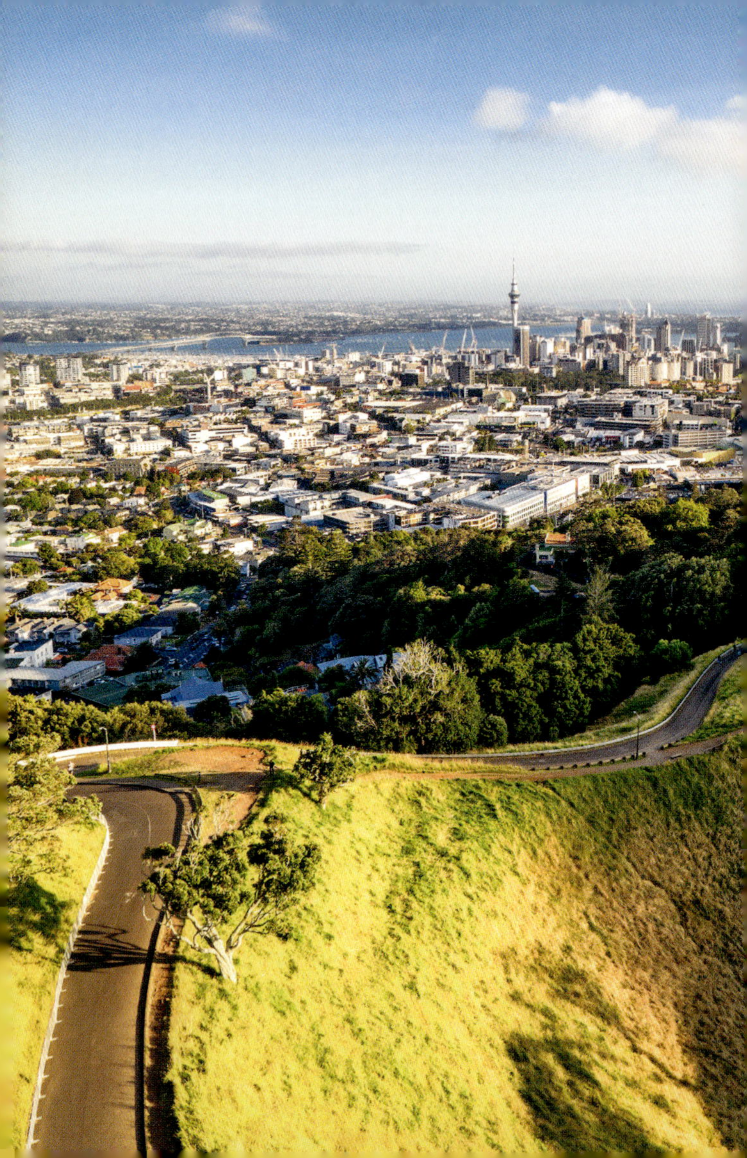

Explore ✦
Kingsland & Mt Eden

Framing the excellent urban views from Auckland's highest volcanic cone, the adjacent heritage suburbs of Kingsland and Mt Eden are popular eating and drinking destinations. A proliferation of the city's best craft-beer venues makes up the Auckland Beer Mile, while throughout the year rugby and cricket at Eden Park attract the city's sports fans.

The Short List

- ***Mt Eden (p60)*** *Soaking up the panoramic views atop the city's tallest volcanic cone.*

- ***Eden Garden (p64)*** *Negotiating a route through this fragrance-infused haven on the slopes of Mt Eden.*

- ***Galbraith's Alehouse (p66)*** *Enjoying NZ craft brews along the Auckland Beer Mile.*

- ***Morningside Precinct (p65)*** *Offering everything from plant-based and sustainable dining to local cider and authentic dumplings.*

- ***Eden Park (p67)*** *Cheering for the Blues, All Blacks or Black Caps at Auckland's home of rugby and cricket.*

Getting There & Around

🚌 Catch bus 27 from Britomart to Mt Eden village. En route alight at stop 1870 to start the walk up Mt Eden.

🚆 Kingsland is a stop on the Western line train service travelling from Britomart to Swanson.

🚶 From Kingsland it's about 300m to Eden Park.

Kingsland & Mt Eden Map on p62

View from Mt Eden (p60) GEORGECLERK/GETTY IMAGES ©

Top Sight
Mt Eden

From the top of Auckland's highest volcanic cone (196m), the entire isthmus and both harbours are laid bare. The symmetrical crater (50m deep) is known as Te Ipu Kai a Mataaho (the Food Bowl of Mataaho, the god of things hidden in the ground). In Māori, Mt Eden is called Maungawhau (mountain of the whau tree).

◉ MAP P62, G5

Maungawhau
250 Mt Eden Rd

Maungawhau's Māori Heritage

The crater of Maungawhau is considered *tapu* (sacred). Do not enter it, but feel free to explore the remainder of the mountain. The remains of *pā* (fortified settlement) terraces and food storage pits are clearly visible.

In 2014, a Treaty of Waitangi settlement with the 13 Tāmaki Makaurau *iwi* (Māori tribes) of Auckland saw the volcanic cone officially named Maungawhau/Mt Eden and ownership vested in the *iwi*, who now jointly manage it with the Auckland Council for the benefit of all Aucklanders.

Accessing Mt Eden

Paths lead up the mountain from six different directions. The walk only takes around 15 minutes, depending on your fitness. Catching bus 27 from Britomart to stop 1870 near Tahaki Reserve is recommended.

An Elephant on Mt Eden

The summit of Mt Eden was vital in the town planning of the city, and the trig (surveying) station still atop the mountain was used as a reference point to draw up surrounding heritage suburbs including Epsom and Mt Eden. Bluestone basalt from quarries around the volcanic scoria cone was harnessed for the construction of nearby Mt Eden prison in the late 19th century.

In 1870 Tom, a three-year-old Indian elephant, was gifted to Queen Victoria's son Prince Alfred during his travels to Auckland, and the Prince's pachyderm hauled basalt up to the peak to construct the trig station so important in Auckland's initial planning.

During his month-long stay in Auckland, the hardworking Tom was apparently rewarded with buns and sweets and even enjoyed a few cold beers in the fledgling city's pubs.

★ Top Tips

- It used to be possible to drive right up to the summit, but concerns over erosion have seen vehicle access restricted to travellers with limited mobility.

- Mt Eden is a stop on the Blue Route of the Auckland Hop On, Hop Off Explorer (p53) bus departing from near Viaduct Harbour.

✗ Take a Break

Mt Eden village is a popular eating and drinking area, and also has some good shopping. Recharge with a craft beer on the leafy outdoor terrace at **Garden Shed** (09-630 3393; www.thegardenshed.kiwi; 470 Mount Eden Rd; mains $18-34; 11am-late Mon-Fri, from 8.30am Sat & Sun).

62

Kingsland & Mt Eden

GREY LYNN

ARCH HILL

KINGSLAND

Eden Park

MORNINGSIDE

For reviews see
- Top Sights — p60
- Sights — p64
- Eating — p64
- Drinking — p66
- Entertainment — p67
- Shopping — p67

0 — 400 m
0 — 0.2 miles

E
F
G
H
NEWTON
Newton Rd
Devon St
France St
Symonds St
Grafton Rd
Carlton Gore Rd
1
NEWMARKET
Khyber Pass Rd
Southern Mwy
2
9
13
Ian McKinnon Dr
EDEN
TERRACE
Mt Eden Rd
Nugent Rd
Boston Rd
2
Mt Eden
8
Enfield St
EPSOM
Porters St
Edwin St
Normanby Rd
Mt Eden Rd
Wynyard St
Clive Rd
3
Coast to Coast Walkway
View Rd
Bellevue Rd
Eden
Gardens
Grenfell Pl
4
Horoeka Ave
Sherbourne St
Esplanade Rd
1
Eden
Garden
Omana
Ave
Woodford Rd
Pentland Ave
MT EDEN
Mt Eden
5
Owens Rd
Prospect Tce
Valley Rd
Oaklands Rd
4
6
3
14
Stokes Rd
Grange Rd
Marama St
6
E
F
G
H

Sights

Eden Garden
GARDENS

1 ⊙ MAP P62, H4

On Mt Eden's rocky eastern slopes, this mature garden is noted for its camellias, rhododendrons and azaleas. (☏09-638 8395; www.edengarden.co.nz; 24 Omana Ave; adult/child $12/free; ⊙9am-4pm)

Eating

French Cafe
FRENCH $$$

2 ⊗ MAP P62, G1

The French Cafe has been rated one of Auckland's top restaurants for more than 30 years. Now helmed by one of Auckland's finest chefs, Sid Sahrawat, there's a subtle and seamless blending of French, Asian and Pacific cuisine. Foraged ingredients regularly feature, as do excellent vegetarian à-la-carte and tasting-menu options. (☏09-377 1911; www.sidatthefrenchcafe.co.nz; 210 Symonds St; mains $36-48, 5-/7-course tasting menus $140/180; ⊙ 6pm-late Tue-Sat)

Zool Zool
JAPANESE $

3 ⊗ MAP P62, G6

A coproduction between two of Auckland's most respected Japanese chefs, Zool Zool is a stylish and modern take on a traditional izakaya (Japanese pub). Some of the city's best ramen noodle dishes are underpinned by hearty and complex broths, and dishes made for sharing over frosty mugs of Japanese beer include tempura squid, soft-shell crab and panko-crumbed fried chicken. (☏09-630 4445; www.zoolzool.co.nz; 405 Mt Eden Rd; snacks $10-18, ramen $15-19; ⊙11.30am-2pm & 5.30-10pm Tue-Sun)

Pasta & Cuore
ITALIAN $$

4 ⊗ MAP P62, G6

Traditional Italian flavours inspired by the cuisine of Bologna shine at this friendly neighbourhood eatery. Secure a table in the rear garden and feast on plump tortellini pasta, and cheese and charcuterie platters perfect for sharing. Takeaway fresh pasta is available, and there's a good selection of natural and organic wines. Book ahead. (☏09-630 9130; www.pastaecuore.co.nz; 409 Mt Eden Rd; mains $23-30; ⊙11am-9pm; ⌘)

Frasers
CAFE $$

One of Mt Eden's most loved cafes (see 14 Map p62, G6) has been reborn after a stylish makeover. The coffee and cakes are still great – especially the baked New York cheesecake – but now wine and craft beer partner the menu of comfort-food classics. Try the mushrooms on sourdough for breakfast, or go for the veal schnitzel with crispy potato gratin for dinner. (☏09-630 6825; www.frasers.nz; cnr Mt Eden & Stokes Rds; mains $15-30; ⊙6am-11pm Mon-Fri, 7am-11pm Sat & Sun)

Morningside Precinct

FOOD HALL $$

5 MAP P62, A4

An easy 300m stroll from Morningside train station, this former curtain factory is now a versatile eating and drinking destination. Highlights include Kind Eatery, specialising in sustainably sourced and plant-based dishes; Bo's Dumplings, a hole-in-the-wall recreation of downtown Shanghai; and Morningcider's compact bar pouring zingy craft ciders. The Morningside Tavern is popular before and after rugby at nearby Eden Park. (www.morningside.nz; 14-18 McDonald St; snacks & mains $8-36; hours vary;)

Xoong

ASIAN $$

6 MAP P62, G6

Pan-Asian shared plates at the stylish Xoong include smoked salmon in a Vietnamese-style curry, Wagyu beef with Thai basil, and kimchi dumplings with shiitake mushrooms. Kick the evening off with cocktails or craft beers from Auckland's Hallertau and Sawmill breweries in Xoong's adjacent bar. (www.xoong.co.nz; 424 Mt Eden Rd; shared plates $11-32; noon-late Wed-Sun, from 5pm Tue;)

Atomic Roastery

CAFE $

7 MAP P62, C3

Java hounds should follow their noses to this, one of the country's best-known coffee roasters. Tasty

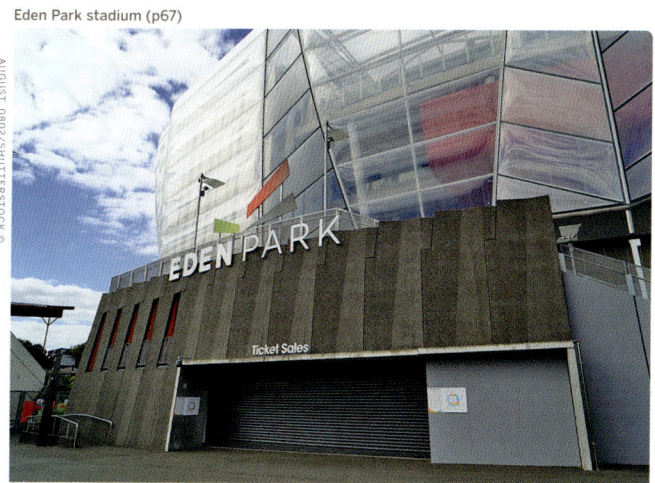

Eden Park stadium (p67)

accompaniments include pies served in mini frying pans, bagels, salads and cakes. (📞0800 286 642; www.atomiccoffee.co.nz; 420c New North Rd; snacks & meals $6-17; ⏰7am-3pm Mon-Fri, from 8am Sat & Sun)

Brothers Juke Joint BBQ
BARBECUE $

8 ❌ MAP P62, F2

A spin-off from central Auckland's excellent Brothers Beer (p92) craft-beer bar, Juke Joint BBQ serves up Southern US–style barbecue in a hip renovated warehouse. Retro 1960s furniture informs the decor, and the compact kids' play area is popular with local families on weekend afternoons.

A Crafty Walking Route

Taking in seven craft-beer destinations, including Galbraith's Alehouse, Brothers Juke Joint BBQ and the Garage Project Cellar Door, the **Auckland Beer Mile** (www.facebook.com/aucklandbeermile) is actually around 3km long and a convenient way to navigate a walking route around some of the city's best destinations for travelling hopheads. Check the Facebook page for regular events at the various bars and taprooms, including food trucks, new beer launches and tap takeovers. Buses also run the route's full extent.

Brothers' own brews are joined by the best from other Kiwi breweries on the gleaming taps. (📞09-638 7592; www.jukejoint.co.nz; 5 Akiraho St; snacks & mains $10-25; ⏰11.30am-10pm Tue-Sat, to 8pm Sun; 👶)

Drinking

Galbraith's Alehouse
BREWERY

9 🍺 MAP P62, G1

Brewing real ales and lagers on site, this cosy English-style pub in a grand heritage building offers bliss on tap. There are always more craft beers from around NZ and the world on the guest taps, and the food's also very good. From April to September, Galbraith's Sunday roast is one of Auckland's best. (📞09-379 3557; http://alehouse.co.nz; 2 Mt Eden Rd; ⏰noon-11pm)

Garage Project Cellar Door
CRAFT BEER

10 🍺 MAP P62, D3

Discover some of NZ's most innovative craft beers at the Auckland outpost of Wellington's Garage Project. Due to the cellar door's licence, beers are served in six-brew tasting trays ($20), and there are always 12 different beers on tap. GP's full range of beers and wild fermented wines are available to take away, and bar snacks include cheese-and-kimchi toasted sandwiches. (https://garageproject.co.nz/pages/kingsland-cellar-door; 357 New North Rd; ⏰noon-8pm Tue, Wed & Sun, to 9pm Thu, 11am-9pm Fri & Sat)

Citizen Park
BEER GARDEN

11 MAP P62, C3

The easy breezy beer-garden vibe of Citizen Park makes it a top spot to meet friends over a few cold ones, before kicking on to a rugby match at nearby Eden Park or for dinner in the adjacent Kingsland restaurant strip. Lots of tap beers, punchy cocktails and a top wine list combine with a decent Mexican-accented menu. (09-846 4964; www.citizenpark.co.nz; 424 New North Rd; 11.30am-late)

Portland Public House
BAR

12 MAP P62, C3

With mismatched furniture, cartoon-themed art and lots of hidden nooks and crannies, the Portland Public House is like spending a few lazy hours at a trendy mate's place. It's also an excellent location for live music. (www.facebook.com/theportlandpublichouse; 463 New North Rd; 4pm-midnight Mon-Wed, to 2am Thu & Fri, noon-2am Sat, noon-midnight Sun)

Entertainment

Power Station
LIVE MUSIC

13 MAP P62, G2

Midrange venue popular with up-and-coming overseas acts and established Kiwi bands. (www.powerstation.net.nz; 33 Mt Eden Rd)

C'mon the Mighty All Blacks

Eden Park (Map p62, C4; 09-815 5551; www.edenpark.co.nz; Reimers Ave) stadium hosts top rugby (winter) and cricket (summer) tests by the All Blacks (www.allblacks.com) and the Black Caps (www.blackcaps.co.nz), respectively. It's also the home ground of Auckland Rugby, the Blues Super Rugby team and Auckland Cricket. Catch the train from Britomart to Kingsland and follow the crowds.

Shopping

Time Out
BOOKS

14 MAP P62, G6

One of the shopping highlights of Mt Eden Village is this excellent independent bookshop with a broad selection of NZ-themed books and always-interesting window displays. (09-630 3331; www.timeout.co.nz; 432 Mt Eden Rd; 9am-9pm)

Royal Jewellery Studio
JEWELLERY

15 MAP P62, C3

Work by local artisans, including beautiful Māori designs and authentic *pounamu* (greenstone) jewellery. (09-846 0200; www.royaljewellerystudio.com; 486 New North Rd; 10am-4pm Tue-Sun)

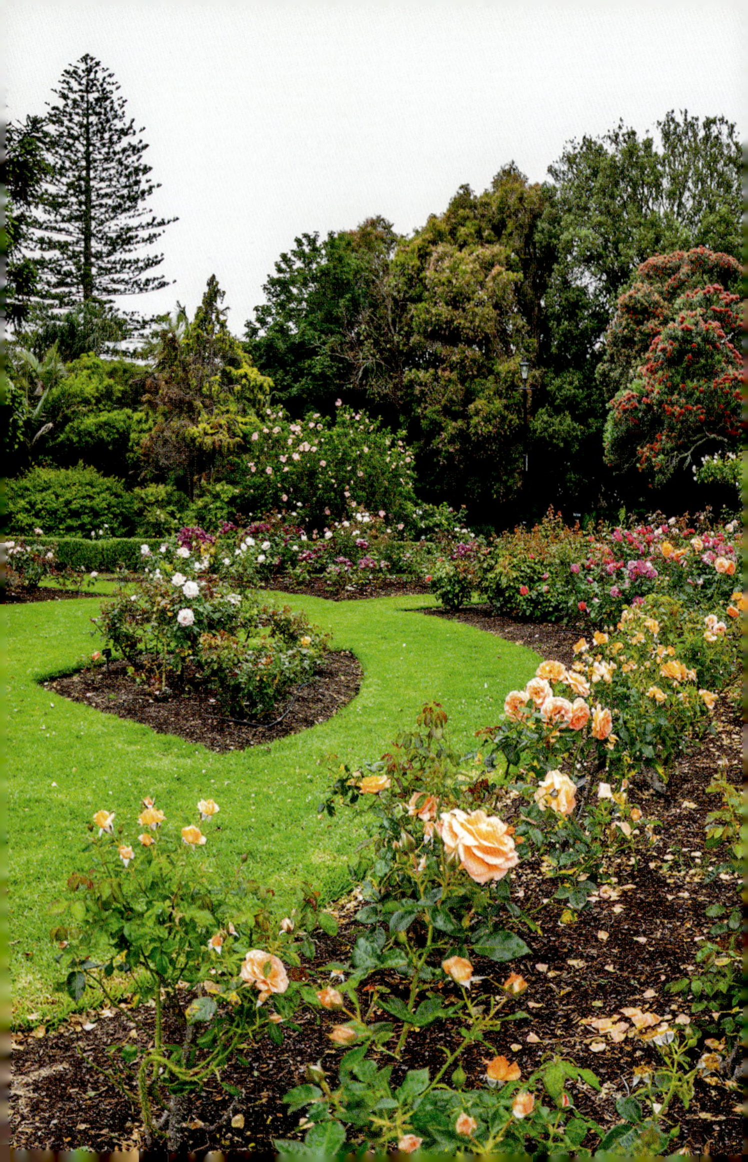

Explore
Parnell & Newmarket

Bordered by the verdant Auckland Domain and the stately Auckland Museum, Parnell is one of Auckland's oldest areas, and amid the cafes, restaurants and up-scale retailers are heritage buildings, including historic churches and 19th-century residences. To the south, Newmarket is a busy shopping precinct known for its fashion boutiques, good cafes and spectacular rooftop dining atop Auckland's newest shopping mall.

The Short List

- **Auckland Museum (p70)** Being awed by the Māori taonga (treasures) at this heritage institution.
- **Auckland Domain (p74)** Relaxing amid the gardens of this expansive green space.
- **Parnell Rose Garden (p74)** Combining an excellent floral display with harbour views.
- **St Mary's Church (p74)** Admiring this fine Gothic Revival church.
- **La Cigale (p76)** Snacking on a Sunday morning at Auckland's best farmers market.

Getting There & Around

🚌 From Britomart, the InnerLink bus travels through Parnell, Newmarket, Karangahape Rd and Ponsonby.

🚆 Newmarket station is a stop on the Southern, Western and Onehunga lines, all beginning at Britomart.

🚶 From Parnell, it's a pleasant walk of around 800m to Auckland Museum and the Auckland Domain.

Parnell & Newmarket Map on p72

Parnell Rose Garden (p74) NATALIA RAMIREZ ROMAN/SHUTTERSTOCK ©

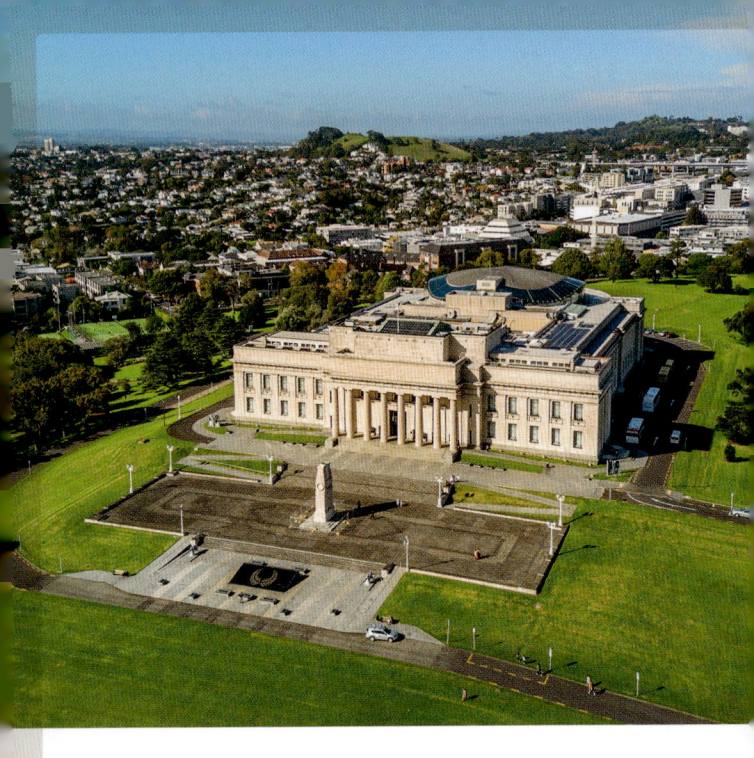

Top Sight 📷
Auckland Museum

This imposing neoclassical temple (1929), whose Noel Lane–designed Grand Atrium is capped with an impressive copper-and-glass dome (2007), dominates the Auckland Domain and is a prominent part of the Auckland skyline, especially when viewed from the harbour. You can purchase admission packages which incorporate a highlights tour.

🎯 MAP P72, C4
📞 09-309 0443
www.aucklandmuseum.com
Auckland Domain
adult/child $25/10
🕙 10am-5pm

An Excellent Māori Collection

The displays of Pacific Island and Māori artefacts on the museum's ground floor are essential viewing. Highlights include a 25m war canoe and an extant carved meeting house (remove your shoes before entering). Enquire about admission packages, which also include a heartfelt Māori cultural performance.

Remembering Wartime Sacrifice

The upper floors of the museum showcase military displays, fulfilling the building's dual role as a war memorial. Especially poignant are the Sicilian marble walls of the WWI and WWII Halls of Memories, inscribed with the names of Aucklanders who died in battle overseas. Remembering the tragic Gallipoli campaign of 1915–16, Auckland's main Anzac commemorations take place at dawn on 25 April at the cenotaph in the museum's forecourt.

Geological History

The unique geological history of NZ – including the time around 100 million years ago when the islands split off from the megacontinent of Gondwana – are showcased in the museum's Origins gallery.

Kids & Volcanic Cones

The museum also has a fascinating display on Auckland's volcanic field, including an eruption simulation, and for younger travellers the Weird & Wonderful Gallery is an opportunity to explore the natural world through interactive discovery stations.

★ Top Tips

○ Auckland Museum and the Domain can be reached on the Auckland Hop On, Hop Off Explorer (p53) sightseeing bus.

○ Online, see www.aucklandmuseum.com/visit/whats-on for details of visiting exhibitions and an always-interesting programme of talks, special events and occasional live-music events.

✕ Take a Break

A handy stop when visiting the nearby Auckland Domain and Auckland Museum, **Billy** (☎09-302 0995; www.billycafe.co.nz; 79 Carlton Gore Rd; mains $10-17; ⏱7am-3.30pm Mon-Fri, from 8am Sat & Sun; 🌱) offers excellent coffee, healthy juices and smoothies, and subtle twists on cafe fare like kimchi nachos.

Parnell & Newmarket

F
- Parnell Baths 8
- Judges Bay
- Judge St
- Parnell Rose Garden
- St Georges Bay Rd

E
- Dove-Myer Robinson Park
- 2 Gladstone Rd
- Taurarua Tce
- Avon St
- Stratford St
- Alberon Reserve
- Albert St
- St Stephens Ave
- PARNELL
- Takutai St
- Brighton Rd
- Balfour Rd
- Cleveland Rd
- 13
- 5 Holy Trinity Cathedral
- 3 St Mary's Church
- Cathedral Pl

D
- The Strand
- Farnham St
- Garfield St
- Windsor St
- Scarborough Tce
- 12
- 9 10
- 23
- St Georges Bay Rd
- Birdwood Cres
- York St
- Bradford St
- Earle St
- Bath St
- 11
- Heather St
- Cheshire St
- 19
- Gibraltar Cres

C
- Te Taoa Cres
- Augustus Rd
- Parnell Rise
- Stanley St
- Carlaw Park
- Lower Domain Dr
- Domain Dr
- THE DOMAIN
- Auckland Museum
- Auckland Domain

B
- Waterloo Qd
- Allen Reserve
- Beach Rd
- Wynyard St
- Symonds St
- Auckland University
- ASB Tennis Centre

A
- Kitchener St
- Bowen Ave
- Princes St
- Albert Park
- Alfred St
- Auckland University
- Symonds St
- Grafton Rd
- Park Rd

72

Parnell & Newmarket

For reviews see
- Top Sights p70
- Sights p74
- Eating p75
- Drinking p77
- Entertainment p78
- Shopping p79

500 m / 0.3 miles

Hobson Bay

REMUERA

Laurie Ave
Ayr St
Ewelme Cottage 4
Bassett Rd
Airey Rd
St Marks Rd
Middleton Rd
Remuera Rd
Nuffield St
Parnell Rd
Maunsell Rd
Kinder House 6
Newmarket
Broadway
Carlton Gore Rd
Kent St
Teed St
Eden St
Crowhurst St
Melrose St
Morrow St
Mortimer Pass
Clovernook St
Gillies Ave
Highwic 7
Southern Mwy
Football Rd
Auckland Domain 1
Grandstand Rd
Khyber Pass Rd
Seccombes Rd
NEWMARKET
Mountain Rd/Park Rd
Almorah Rd
EPSOM
Mountain Rd
Outhwaite Park
Grafton
Boston Rd
Southern Mwy
Seafield View Rd
GRAFTON

Sights

Auckland Domain PARK
1 MAP P72, B5

Covering about 80 hectares, this green swathe contains the Auckland Museum (p70), sports fields, interesting sculptures, formal gardens, wild corners and the **Wintergarden** (Wintergarden Rd; admission free; 9am-5.30pm Mon-Sat, to 7.30pm Sun Nov-Mar, 9am-4.30pm Apr-Oct), with its fernery, tropical house, cool house, cute cat statue, coffee kiosk and neighbouring cafe. The mound in the centre of the park is all that remains of Pukekaroa, one of Auckland's volcanoes. At its humble peak, a totara tree surrounded by a palisade honouring the first Māori king. (Domain Dr; 24hr)

Parnell Rose Garden GARDENS
2 MAP P72, E1

These formal gardens are blooming excellent from November to March. A stroll through Dove-Myer Robinson Park leads to peaceful Judges Bay and tiny **St Stephen's Chapel** (Judge St), built for the signing of the constitution of NZ's Anglican Church (1857). (85-87 Gladstone Rd)

St Mary's Church CHURCH
3 MAP P72, E4

Next door to the Holy Trinity Cathedral, this wonderful wooden Gothic Revival church (1886) has a burnished interior and interesting stained-glass windows. (Parnell Rd; 10am-3pm)

Ewelme Cottage HISTORIC BUILDING
4 MAP P72, E5

Built in 1864 for a clergyman, this storybook cottage is an exceptionally well-preserved example of an early colonial house. (09-524 5729; www.historic.org.nz; 14 Ayr St; adult/child $8.50/free; 10.30am-4.30pm Sun)

Holy Trinity Cathedral CHURCH
5 MAP P72, E4

Auckland's Anglican cathedral is a hodgepodge of architectural styles, especially compared to St Mary's Church next door. Holy Trinity's windows are also notable, especially the rose window by English artist Carl Edwards, which is particularly striking above the simple kauri altar. (09-303 9500; www.holy-trinity.org.nz; cnr St Stephens Ave & Parnell Rd; 10am-3pm)

Kinder House HISTORIC BUILDING
6 MAP P72, D5

Built of volcanic stone, this 1857 home displays the watercolours and memorabilia of the Reverend Dr John Kinder (1819–1903), headmaster of the Church of England Grammar School. (09-379 4008; www.kinder.org.nz; 2 Ayr St; admission by donation; noon-3pm Wed-Sun)

Highwic HISTORIC BUILDING
7 MAP P72, C8

A marvellous Carpenter Gothic house (1862), sitting amid lush, landscaped grounds. (09-524

5729; www.historic.org.nz; 40 Gillies Ave; adult/child $10/free; ⏲10.30am-4.30pm Wed-Sun)

Parnell Baths SWIMMING
8 MAP P72, F1

Outdoor saltwater pools with an awesome 1950s mural. (☏09-373 3561; www.parnellbaths.co.nz; Judges Bay Rd; adult/child $6.40/free; ⏲6am-8pm Mon-Fri, 8am-8pm Sat & Sun Nov-Easter)

Eating

Gerome GREEK $$
9 MAP P72, D3

Greek cuisine is rare in Auckland, but Gerome's modern interpretation of traditional Hellenic flavours make it one of Auckland's best restaurants. Highlights include the pork and lamb *manti* (dumplings) with fermented chilli, and the superb slow-roasted lamb kleftiko with watermelon jelly and pine nuts. On a warm summer's afternoon or evening, sit in the open-air pavilion out front. (☏09-373 3883; www.gerome.nz; 269 Parnell Rd; shared plates $14-34; ⏲11.30am-late)

Pasture MODERN NZ $$$
10 MAP P72, D3

Pasture is unlike any other dining experience in the city. You'll need to book a few months ahead – the compact space has just two seatings per night and room for only six diners – to enjoy chef Verner's intensely seasonal multicourse menu harnessing foraging, fermentation and wood-fired cooking.

Wintergarden, Auckland Domain

Look forward to an eclectic soundtrack, also of the chef's choosing. (☎09-300 5077; www.pastureakl.com; 3/235 Parnell Rd; menu per person $230; ⏲5.45pm-late Wed-Sun; 🚇)

Han KOREAN $$

11 🍴 MAP P72, D2

Korean flavours continue to influence Auckland's dining scene, and Han's evolution from a food truck to a standalone restaurant is testament to the innovation of chef Min Baek. Lunch is a more informal affair – think Korean-style burgers and healthy rice bowls – but the dinner menu really shines with modern dishes, including beef short rib with beetroot and asparagus. (☎09-377 0977; www.hanrestaurant.co.nz; 100 Parnell Rd; mains $30-41; ⏲11am-2.30pm Wed-Sat, 5.30-11pm Wed-Sun)

Woodpecker Hill FUSION $$$

12 🍴 MAP P72, D2

Marrying the flavours and shared dining style of Southeast Asian cuisine with an American approach to meat (smoky slow-cooked brisket, sticky short ribs etc), this odd bird has pecked out a unique place on the Auckland dining scene. The decor – a riotous mishmash of tartan, faux fur, copper bells and potted plants – is as eclectic as the food. (☎09-309 5055; www.woodpeckerhill.co.nz; 196 Parnell Rd; large dishes $32-42; ⏲noon-late)

La Cigale MARKET $

13 🍴 MAP P72, E2

Catering to Francophile foodies, this warehouse stocks French imports and has a patisserie-laden cafe. During the weekend farmers markets, this *cigale* (cicada) really chirps, offering stalls laden with local artisan produce and a fine array of ethnic treats from recent arrivals to the city. (☎09-366 9361; www.lacigale.co.nz; 69 St Georges Bay Rd; cafe $10-21; ⏲9am-3pm Wed-Fri, to 1.30pm Sat & Sun)

&Sushi SUSHI $$

14 🍴 MAP P72, C7

There's definitely no shortage of places to buy sushi around Auckland, but &Sushi definitely stands out from the competition with innovative and artfully presented rolls. Mix and match a plate with rolls made with natural brown rice, edible flowers and kimchi-studded pork, or order one of &Sushi's lunch offerings. Our favourite is the tuna and salmon poké on quinoa. (☎09-523-4223; www.andsushi.co.nz; 12 Teed St; sushi from $3, mains $16-22; ⏲9am-3.30pm Sun-Wed, to 8.30pm Thu-Sat)

Winona Forever CAFE $$

Some of Auckland's best counter food – including stonking cream doughnuts – partners with innovative cafe culture at this always-busy eatery (see 11 🍴 Map p72, D2) near good shopping and art galleries along Parnell Rd. Locals crowd in with travellers for coffee, craft beer and wine, and one of the cafe's signature dishes: the tempura soft-shell-crab omelette. (☏09-974 2796; www.winonaforever.co.nz; 100 Parnell Rd; mains $20-26; ⏱7am-4pm Mon-Fri, from 8am Sat & Sun)

Little & Friday CAFE $

15 ✗ MAP P72, B6

Renowned for some of Auckland's best homestyle baking, the sleek and modern Little & Friday is worth the 500m stroll from Newmarket's main shopping street. Try the cardamom-and-coconut vanilla porridge with poached pear. Pro tip: the best doughnuts in town usually arrive in store around 10.30am from the external commercial kitchen. (☏09-524 8742; www.littleandfriday.com; 11 McColl St; snacks & mains $10-22; ⏱7am-3.30pm Mon-Fri, 8am-4pm Sat & Sun)

Teed Street Larder CAFE $$

16 ✗ MAP P72, C7

Polished concrete floors, beer-crate tables and colourful oversized lampshades set the scene. There are plenty of enticing cooked items on the menu, but it's hard to go past the delicious sandwiches and tarts. Fresh baking emerges from the ovens throughout the day. (☏09-524 8406; www.teedstreetlarder.co.nz; 7 Teed St; mains $14-27; ⏱7am-4pm Mon-Fri, from 8am Sat & Sun)

Newmarket Rooftop Dining 🍽

Opened in late 2019, the rooftop dining precinct of the expanded and refurbished Westfield Newmarket (p79) shopping mall is a versatile affair with various cafes and restaurants offering everything from Peruvian cuisine to artisan gelato and Asian-fusion shared plates. In the same complex is a good food court with Japanese, Malaysian and Greek flavours.

Hansan VIETNAMESE $

17 ✗ MAP P72, C8

A branch of a small local chain serving good-value, authentic Vietnamese food. (☏09-523 3988; www.hansan.co.nz; 55 Nuffield St; mains $12-18; ⏱11am-10pm)

Drinking

Lumsden CRAFT BEER

18 🍺 MAP P72, C6

A shrine to craft beers from around NZ, the Lumsden's outdoor terrace is a good spot to relax after exploring Newmarket's shops. Foureen different beers are always on tap – check the website for the current selection – and partner with decent pub food such as tacos and pizza. For a smartphone-free time, head to the Digital Detox Space. (☏09-550 1201; www.thelumsden.co.nz; 444 Khyber Pass Rd; ⏱11.30am-midnight)

Pineapple on Parnell
COCKTAIL BAR

19 MAP P72, D3

Push open the door decorated with a chunky brass pineapple to discover this elegant bar with leather furniture and a gentlemen's-club ambience. Savvy bartenders concoct interesting cocktails – try the citrusy Imperial Blush with gin, Aperol, pink grapefruit juice and orange marmalade – and snack on cheese and charcuterie boards if you're peckish. (09-336 1827; www.facebook.com/pineappleonparnell; 207 Parnell Rd; 5pm-late Wed-Sat)

Doolan Brothers
IRISH PUB

20 MAP P72, C6

This spacious, friendly and longstanding Irish pub is a grand place to watch live sport. Keep an eye on the match schedules of the All Blacks and the Auckland Blues (rugby union), the New Zealand Warriors (rugby league) and the New Zealand Breakers (basketball). Drinks-wise, there's a good selection of decent beers from Kiwi breweries, including Emersons and Panhead. (09-529 2485; www.doolanbrothers.co.nz; 414 Khyber Pass Rd; 11.30am-late)

Entertainment

Rialto
CINEMA

21 MAP P72, C7

Mainly art-house and international films, plus better mainstream fare and regular specialist film festivals. (09-369 2417; www.rialto.co.nz; 167 Broadway)

La Cigale (76)

Shopping

Poi Room
ART

22 MAP P72, C7

An excellent showcase of work by NZ artists and designers, including prints, paintings, ceramics, jewellery and homewares. Many of the items for sale reference Māori and Pasifika themes. (☎09-520 0399; www.thepoiroom.co.nz; 17 Osborne St; ⏱9.30am-5.30pm Mon-Fri, to 5pm Sat, 10am-4pm Sun)

Zambesi
CLOTHING

23 MAP P72, D3

Zambesi, among the most famous fashion labels to come out of NZ, is much sought after by local and international celebs. (☎09-308 0363; www.zambesi.co.nz; 287 Parnell Rd; ⏱10am-6pm Mon-Fri, 11am-5pm Sat & Sun)

Kate Sylvester
CLOTHING

24 MAP P72, C7

One of NZ's most respected designers, Kate Sylvester's playful and stylish designs often feature interesting and vibrant fabrics. (☎09-524 8872; www.katesylvester.co.nz; 1 Teed St; ⏱9.30am-5.30pm Mon-Thu, to 6pm Fri, 10am-5pm Sat, 11am-4pm Sun)

Huffer
CLOTHING

25 MAP P72, C8

Stylish technical apparel and streetwear from a hip NZ company with its roots in snowboarding and skateboarding. (www.huffer.co.nz; 309 Broadway; ⏱9am-7pm Mon-Wed, Fri & Sat, to 9pm Thu, 10am-7pm Sun)

Westfield Newmarket
MALL

26 MAP P72, C7

Auckland's newest and most upmarket mall features rooftop dining and a good food court. (www.westfield.co.nz/newmarket; Broadway; ⏱shops 9am-7pm)

Creative & Brave
ARTS & CRAFTS

27 MAP P72, C8

A diverse and interesting range of gifts, arts and crafts from NZ designers. (☎09-600 1346; www.creativeandbrave.co.nz; 277 Broadway Newmarket; ⏱9am-7pm Mon-Wed & Sat, to 9pm Thu & Fri, 10am-7pm Sun)

Summer's Hottest Ticket

Attending the women's and men's tournaments of the ASB Tennis Classic, held across consecutive weeks in January at the **ASB Tennis Centre** (Map p72, B2; www.tennisauckland.co.nz; 1 Tennis Lane), is a popular way for many Aucklanders to begin the year. There's usually a smattering of the world's top 20 players, as the Auckland tournaments are used as a warm-up event before February's Australian Open.

Top Sight 📷
One Tree Hill

The volcanic cone of One Tree Hill (Maungakiekie) was the isthmus' key Māori pā (fortress) and the greatest in New Zealand. At the top (182m) there are 360-degree views and the grave of John Logan Campbell, who gifted the land to the city in 1901 and requested that a memorial be built to the Māori people on the summit.

★ Getting There

🚌 Catch bus 309 from Civic Theatre to stop 8714 on Manukau Rd. Walk 1km east on Greenlane Rd.

🚗 Take Greenlane exit off Southern Motorway and turn right into Green Lane West.

One Tree to Rule Them All

Looking at One Tree Hill, your first thought will probably be, 'Where's the bloody tree?' Good question. Up until 2000 a Monterey pine stood at the top of the hill. This was a replacement for a sacred totara that was chopped down by British settlers in 1852. Māori activists first attacked the foreign usurper in 1994, finishing the job in 2000.

After much consultation with local Māori and tree experts, a grove of six pohutukawa and three totara trees was planted on the summit in mid-2016. In an arboreal version of the *X-Factor*, the weaker-performing trees will be eliminated, with only one tree left standing by 2026.

Playtime & the Planets

Near an excellent children's playground, the **Stardome** (09-624 1246; www.stardome.org.nz; 670 Manukau Rd; shows adult/child from $12/10; 10am-5pm Mon, to 9.30pm Tue-Thu, to 11pm Fri-Sun) offers regular stargazing and planetarium shows (usually 7pm and 8pm Wednesday to Sunday, with extra shows on weekends) that aren't dependent on Auckland's fickle weather.

The U2 Connection

Auckland's most beloved landmark achieved international recognition in 1987 when U2 released the song 'One Tree Hill' on their acclaimed *Joshua Tree* album. It was only released as a single in NZ, where it went to number one for six weeks. The song was written as a tribute to Greg Carroll, a Kiwi who was a roadie for the band, and tragically died in a motorcycle accident in Dublin in 1986.

★ Top Tips

○ The slopes of One Tree Hill and the pastures of Cornwall Park are still a working farm, and from July to September, newborn lambs and calves are a common sight. Spring daffodils enliven the park's avenues.

○ Cornwall Park is perfect for a picnic with many well-established trees providing shade. There are also tables and coin-operated gas barbecues.

○ Allow time to explore Cornwall Park's historic Acacia Cottage (1841).

○ Cornwall Park Information Centre has fascinating interactive displays illustrating what the *pā* would have looked like when 5000 people lived here.

✕ Take a Break

In surrounding Cornwall Park, there's a good cafe with a sunny terrace and a popular ice-cream kiosk that's mainly open in spring and summer.

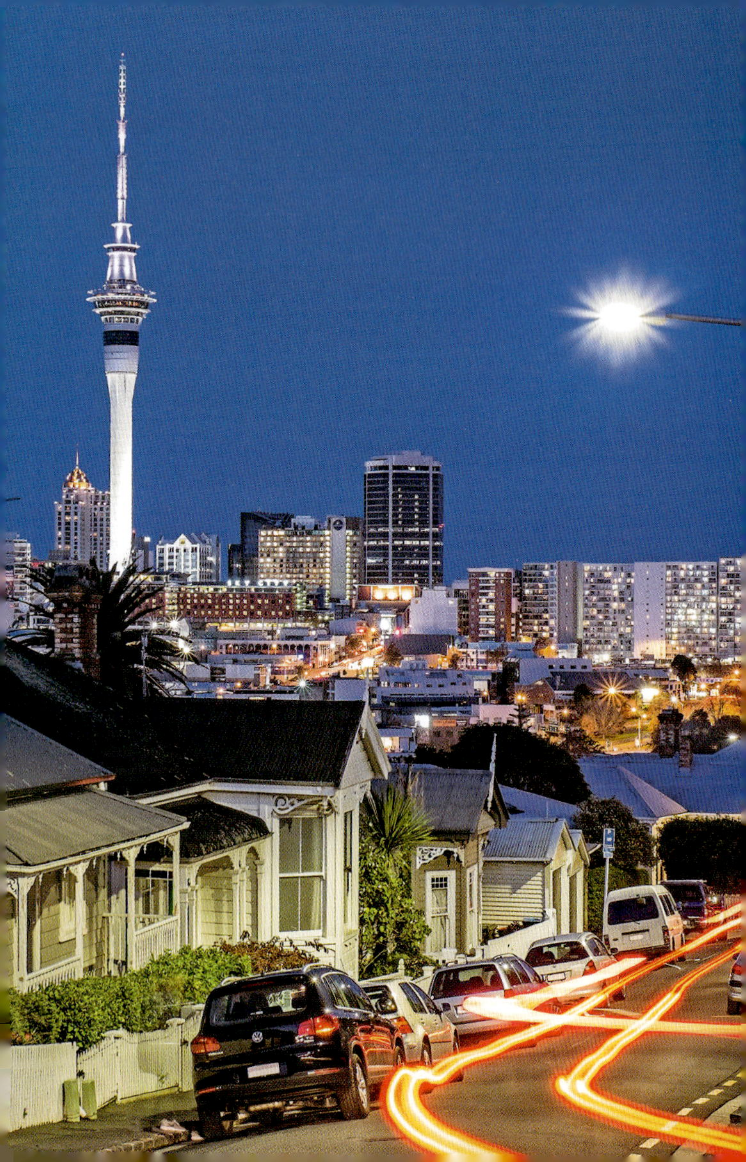

Explore
Ponsonby & Karangahape Road

Two of Auckland's most interesting inner neighbourhoods, Ponsonby and Karangahape Rd feature heritage shopfronts and excellent opportunities for eating and drinking. Colloquially abbreviated to 'K Rd', the more free-spirited of the two is also a hub for vintage shopping and art galleries.

The Short List

- **Ponsonby Central (p84)** Checking out cafes, restaurants and bars amid repurposed warehouses and laneways.

- **St Kevin's Arcade (p94)** Combining interesting shopping with eating and drinking in this refurbished heritage arcade.

- **Sidart (p88)** Enjoying a meal to remember at one of the city's most innovative restaurants.

- **Karangahape Rd (p88)** Hitting the restaurants and bars of Auckland's most interesting up-and-coming dining precinct.

- **Art Galleries (p92)** Undertaking a self-guided walking tour of the area's arts scene.

Getting There & Around

🚌 From Britomart, the InnerLink bus travels on a route taking in Parnell, Newmarket, Karangahape Rd and Ponsonby.

🚶 From Ponsonby it's an interesting, flat walk of around 1.4km to Karangahape Rd.

Ponsonby & Karangahape Rd Map on p86

Ponsonby JOSE ANTONIO MACIEL/GETTY IMAGES ©

Top Sight
Ponsonby Central

Restaurants, cafes, bars and gourmet food shops fill this upmarket former warehouse space offering everything from Auckland's best pizza and Argentinian barbecue to Asian street food partnered with zingy cocktails. It's a prime eating and drinking destination and offers excellent dining options from breakfast right through to dinner.

◉ MAP P86, C5

www.ponsonbycentral.co.nz

136-138 Ponsonby Rd

⏱ 7am-10.30pm Sun-Wed, to midnight Thu-Sat

Blue Breeze Inn

A so-hip-it-hurts **eatery** (☎09-360 0303; www.thebluebreezeinn.co.nz; mains $26-36; ⏱noon-late) where regional Chinese flavours combine with a funky retro Pacific ambience. The waiters are sassy, the rum cocktails are deliciously strong and menu standouts include pork belly and pickled cucumber steamed buns, and cumin-spiced lamb.

Bedford Soda & Liquor

At **Bedford Soda & Liquor** (☎09-378 7362; www.bedfordsodaliquor.co.nz; ⏱noon-midnight), candlelight and a semi-industrial fit-out set the scene for a New York–style bar devoted to the American drinking culture. The cocktails are pricey but worth it: some come wreathed in smoke, others in the alcoholic equivalent of a snow globe.

Bird on a Wire

Tasty sandwiches and healthy burgers, seasonal salads and rotisserie chickens to take away at **Bird on a Wire** (☎09-361 3407; www.birdonawire.co.nz; mains $11-20; ⏱7.30am-late), pictured. Select your baste of choice – Jamaican jerk or truffle butter, perhaps – and you're sorted.

More on the Menu

Ponsonby Central has a tasty menu of other eating and drinking options. **Miss Istanbul** offers Turkish-style street food, while there's quite possibly Auckland's best burgers at **Burger Burger**. Check out **Dante's Pizza** for authentic Neapolitan flavours and **The Dairy** for luscious NZ ice cream and grilled-cheese sandwiches.

★ Top Tips

The surrounding Ponsonby neighbourhood is a good place to stay while visiting Auckland. Accommodation includes luxury B&Bs in heritage wooden villas while Viaduct Harbour and the central city are a downhill stroll or short bus ride away.

✕ Take a Break

For an equally wide range of global flavours – but at more budget-friendly prices than Ponsonby Central – make the short 250m stroll to the **Ponsonby Village International Food Court** (www.ponsonbyfoodcourt.co.nz; 106 Ponsonby Rd; mains $9-20; ⏱11am-10pm; 🍴). Japanese, Malaysian, Chinese, Turkish, Thai, Lao and Indian flavours are all on offer. Beer and wine are well priced.

Ponsonby & Karangahape Road

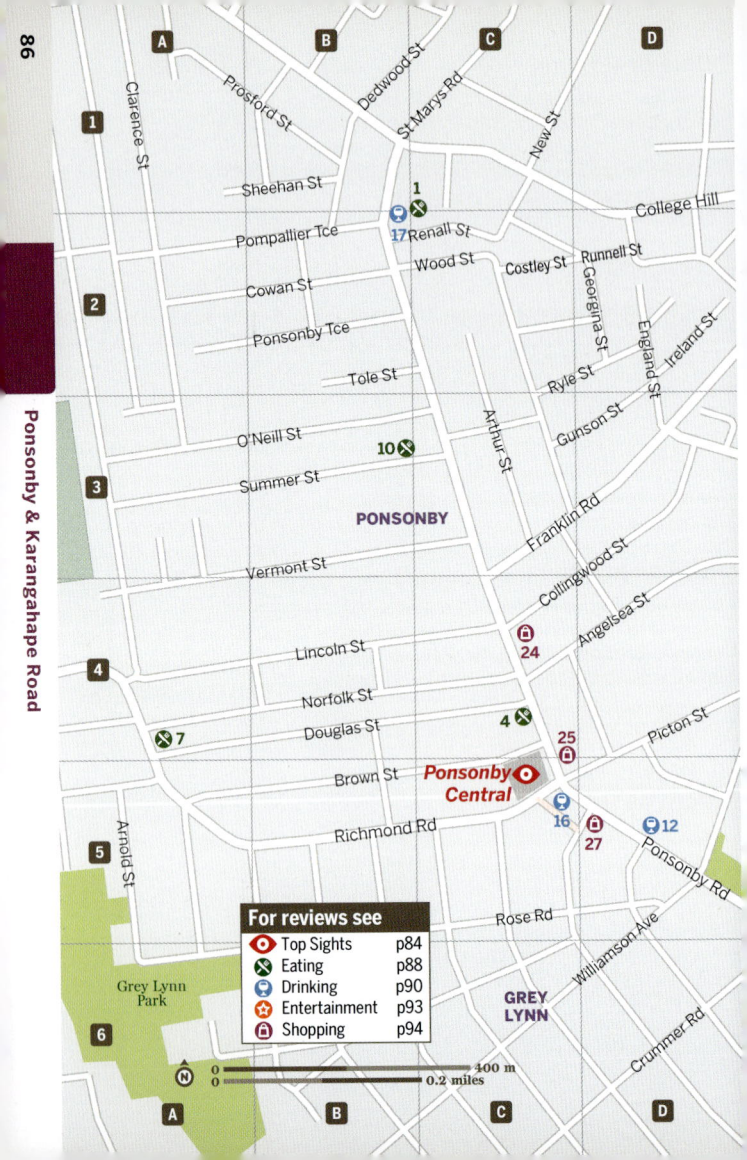

For reviews see

◎	Top Sights	p84
✖	Eating	p88
🍺	Drinking	p90
★	Entertainment	p93
🛍	Shopping	p94

87

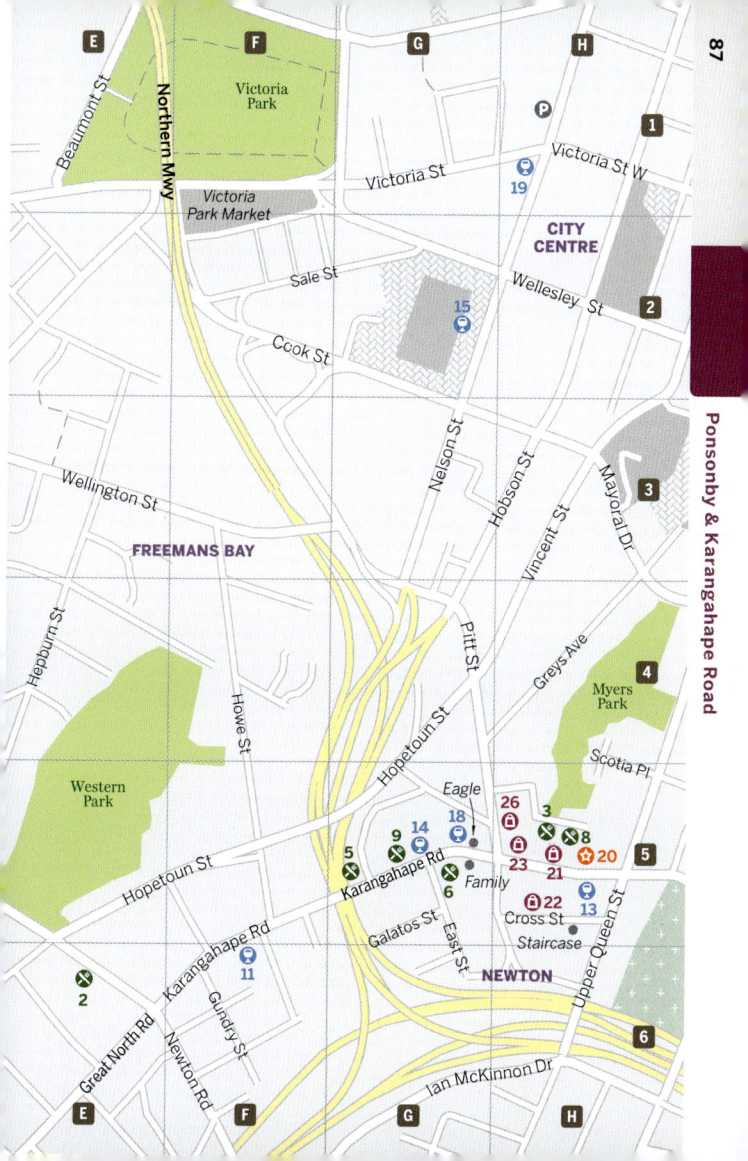

Ponsonby & Karangahape Road

Locations visible on map:

- E: Beaumont St, Hepburn St, Great North Rd
- F: Victoria Park, Victoria Park Market, Sale St, Cook St, Wellington St, FREEMANS BAY, Howe St, Western Park, Hopetoun St, Karangahape Rd, Gundry St, Newton Rd, Northern Mwy
- G: Victoria St, Nelson St, Hobson St, Pitt St, Hopetoun St, Karangahape Rd, Galatos St, East St, NEWTON, Ian McKinnon Dr
- H: Victoria St W, CITY CENTRE, Wellesley St, Vincent St, Mayoral Dr, Greys Ave, Myers Park, Scotia Pl, Cross St Staircase, Upper Queen St

Numbered markers: 2, 3, 5, 6, 8, 9, 11, 13, 14, 15, 18, 19, 20, 21, 22, 23, 26

Labels: Eagle, Family

Eating

Sidart
MODERN NZ $$$

1 MAP P86, C1

No one in Auckland produces creative degustations quite like Sid Sahrawat. It's food as both art and science but, more importantly, food to fire up the taste buds, delight the brain, satisfy the stomach and put a smile on the face. The restaurant is a little hard to find, tucked away at the rear of what was once the Alhambra cinema. (09-360 2122; www.sidart.co.nz; Three Lamps Plaza, 283 Ponsonby Rd; mains $32-38, 5-/7-course tasting menus $125/175; 6pm-late Tue-Sun, noon-3pm Fri)

Azabu
JAPANESE $$

2 MAP P86, E6

Nikkei cuisine, an exciting blend of Japanese and Peruvian influences, is the focus at Azabu. Amid a dramatic interior enlivened by striking images of Tokyo, standout dishes include the tuna sashimi tostada, Japanese tacos with wasabi avocado, and king prawns with a jalapeño-and-ponzu dressing. Arrive early and enjoy a basil- and chilli-infused cachaca cocktail at Azabu's Roji bar. (09-320 5292; www.azabuponsonby.co.nz; 26 Ponsonby Rd; mains & shared plates $16-39; noon-late Wed-Sun, from 5pm Mon & Tue)

Gemmayze St
LEBANESE $$

3 MAP P86, H5

Located amid the restored heritage architecture of St Kevin's Arcade, Gemmayze St presents a stylish update on Lebanese cuisine. Mint, orange-blossom and rosewater cocktails are prepared at the beaten-copper bar, while shared tables encourage lots of sociable dining on meze and expertly grilled meats. The optional 'Jeeb' menu (per person $65) is a brilliant option for a leisurely feast. (09-600 1545; www.gemmayzestreet.co.nz; St Kevin's Arcade, 15/183 Karangahape Rd; meze & mains $10-35; 5.30-10pm Thu-Sat;)

Saan
THAI $$

4 MAP P86, C4

Hot in both senses of the word, this superfashionable restaurant focuses on the fiery cuisine of the Isaan and Lanna regions of northern Thailand. The menu is conveniently sorted from least to most spicy and split into smaller and larger dishes for sharing. Be sure to order the soft-shell crab. (09-320 4237; www.saan.co.nz; 160 Ponsonby Rd; dishes $12-38; 5pm-late daily, noon-3pm Fri)

Cotto
ITALIAN $$

5 MAP P86, G5

Modern Italian cuisine shines at Cotto, a perpetually busy eatery along Karangahape Rd. On the shared-plates menu, highlights include spinach and goats' cheese dumplings with fried sage leaves, and grilled eggplant with whipped feta cheese. Enjoy a cocktail in the ramshackle-chic interior. Queues are frequent on weekends, so aim to get there when it opens. (☎09-394 1555; www.cotto.co.nz; 375 Karangahape Rd; shared plates $16-22; ⊙5pm-late Mon-Sat)

Apero BISTRO $$

6 ✖ MAP P86, G5

House-made terrines, sausages and charcuterie are the culinary stars at Apero, another Karangahape Rd establishment offering the perfect blend of eating and drinking. Service from the co-owner is relaxed but authoritative – expect well-considered wine recommendations. Ease into the brick-lined space knowing everything from the goats' cheese croquettes to the 'Something Fish' seafood special will be damn tasty. (☎09-373 4778; www.apero.co.nz; 280 Karangahape Rd; shared plates $8-25; ⊙4pm-late Wed, Thu, Sat & Sun, from noon Fri)

Lokanta MEDITERRANEAN $$

7 ✖ MAP P86, A4

Featuring the cuisine of the eastern Mediterranean, unpretentious Lokanta is a laid-back alternative to the trendier eateries dotted along nearby Ponsonby Rd. Greek and Turkish flavours happily coexist, and robust Greek wines partner well with hearty dishes, including chargrilled octopus. The

Saan

BRETT ATKINSON/LONELY PLANET ©

coconut-and-almond baklava introduces a tropical influence to the classic dessert. (☏09-360 6355; www.lokanta.nz; 137a Richmond Rd; meze $7-19, mains $27-34; ⏰5pm-late Tue-Sun)

Bestie
CAFE $$

8 ❌ MAP P86, H5

One of the excellent cafes and restaurants in revitalised St Kevin's Arcade, Bestie is a perfect refuelling stop after trawling the arty and vintage shops along Karangahape Rd. Try to secure a table overlooking leafy Myers Park, and pair coffee or kombucha with signature dishes such as Bestie's ricotta doughnuts, or flatbread with chorizo, labneh and a chilli fried egg. (www.bestiecafe.co.nz; St Kevin's Arcade, Karangahape Rd; mains $12-22; ⏰7.30am-3.30pm Mon-Fri, 8.30am-3.30pm Sat & Sun; 🍴)

Fort Greene
CAFE $$

9 ❌ MAP P86, G5

Baked on site, Auckland's best sourdough bread is used for Fort Greene's tasty gourmet sandwiches. Pick some up for a picnic or tuck into the Reuben sandwich with salt-beef brisket and house-made sauerkraut. Great coffee and eggy breakfasts too. (☏022 425 7791; www.fortgreene.co.nz; 327 Karangahape Rd; sandwiches $15-21; ⏰7.30am-4pm Mon-Fri, 8.30am-3.30pm Sat, 9am-3pm Sun; 🍴)

Little Bird Kitchen
CAFE $$

10 ❌ MAP P86, B3

Everything on the menu is prepared raw and uncooked, but is still tasty and healthy. Tuck into dishes studded with acai berries, chia seeds and organic fruit; there are even bagels, risotto, tacos and delicious cakes. For dinner, highlights include pumpkin-and-lemongrass curry and kimchi burgers. The drinks list includes kombucha, juices, smoothies and organic beer. (☏09-555 3278; www.littlebirdorganics.co.nz; 1a Summer St; mains $15-23; ⏰7.30am-4pm daily, 6-9.30pm Wed-Sat; 🍴)

Drinking

Madame George
BAR

11 🍺 MAP P86, F6

Two patron saints of cool – Elvis Presley and Marlon Brando – look down on this compact space. Shoot the breeze with the friendly bar staff over a craft beer or Auckland's best cocktails, or grab a shared table out front and watch the passing theatre of K Rd. It's just like hanging at your hippest mate's place. (☏09-308 9039; www.madamegeorge.co.nz; 490 Karangahape Rd; ⏰5pm-late Tue-Sat)

Deadshot
COCKTAIL BAR

12 🍺 MAP P86, D5

Featuring some of Auckland's most experienced bartenders,

Global Cheap Eats

Before Karangahape Rd's relatively recent emergence as a hotspot for innovative young chefs, it was already well-known as one of Auckland's best areas for good-value food from around the world. Back in the 1980s, the **Little Turkish Cafe** was a pioneer for Middle Eastern food in the city, and it's still going strong more than three decades later. Other K Rd foodie treats to track down include the cashew *barfi* (an Indian sweet) at **Rasoi Vegetarian Restaurant** and the Malaysian-style *roti canai* and beef *rendang* at **Uncle Man's**. For frosty mugs of Japanese beer and steamed buns crammed with pork belly, pull up a chair at **Acho** in St Kevin's Arcade, followed by dessert of a strawberry-and-cornflake sundae just next door at the very hip **Lowbrow**.

Deadshot – cowboy parlance for 'strong booze' – is where you can sample the city's cocktail A-game. With bar stools, brick walls, and cosy and intimate booths, there's also a touch of the Wild West in the decor, but it's still a thoroughly cosmopolitan drinking hole. Expect classic cocktails with a twist. (www.facebook.com/Deadshotnz; 45 Ponsonby Rd; ⊙5pm-2am)

Bar Celeste   WINE BAR
13 MAP P86, H5

Inspired by the 'neo bistro' movement of Paris, Bar Celeste blurs the line between intimate bar and innovative restaurant. Natural wines are regularly featured, there's usually a food-friendly sour beer on the taps, and the menu of seasonal small plates could include sweetbreads, crudo trevally or grilled octopus. Don't miss the superb sourdough bread from K Rd neighbours, Fort Greene. (www.barceleste.com; 146 Karangahape Rd; shared plates $16-32; ⊙3pm-late Tue-Sat)

Lovebucket   COCKTAIL BAR
14 MAP P86, G5

Lovebucket is a more sophisticated alternative to K Rd's often youthful after-dark vibe. Courtesy of shared ownership with the Hallertau Brewery in West Auckland, Lovebucket's craft-beer selection is one of Auckland's best – including barrel-aged and sour beers. Quirky cocktails and a well-informed wine list join interesting bar snacks such as cheeses, charcuterie and gourmet toasted sandwiches. (☎09-869 2469; www.lovebucket.co.nz; K'Road Food Workshop, 309 Karangahape Rd; ⊙4pm-late Tue-Sun)

K Road & Ponsonby Art Scene

Filling the spaces between ethnic restaurants, hip wine bars and vintage clothing shops, Karangahape Rd is home to the highest concentration of studios and art galleries in all of NZ. Neighbouring Ponsonby also includes public and dealer galleries, artist-run spaces and auction houses. See www.kroad.com/arts to download a map outlining different galleries and studios spaces throughout the Karangahape Rd and Ponsonby areas. For some of the area's best street art, check out Cross St, a narrow laneway one block south of Karangahape Rd.

Brothers Beer
CRAFT BEER

15 MAP P86, G2

This beer bar combines quirky decor with 18 taps crammed with Brothers' own brews and guest beers from NZ and further afield. Hundreds more bottled beers are chilling in the fridges, and bar food includes pizza. There are occasional movie and comedy nights, and beers are available to take away. The adjacent City Works Depot has other good eating options. (09-366 6100; www.brothersbeer.co.nz; City Works Depot, 90 Wellesley St; noon-10pm)

Hoppers Garden Bar
BAR

16 MAP P86, C5

Gin and craft beers from around NZ combine with excellent street-food-inspired bar snacks at the summery and relaxed Hoppers Garden Bar. Ponsonby locals crowd in, often with their canine pals, to enjoy zingy cocktails or seasonal brews from Auckland brewing stars like Behemoth and Hallertau. Flavour-packed menu highlights include salmon ceviche and steamed buns with soft-shell crab. (www.hoppersgardenbar.co.nz; 134 Ponsonby Rd; 4pm-late Mon-Wed, from noon Thu-Sun)

Annabel's
WINE BAR

17 MAP P86, B2

A self-described 'neighbourhood bar', Annabel's would also be right at home in the backstreets of Bordeaux or Barcelona. Cheese and charcuterie platters combine with a Eurocentric wine list, while Spanish beers and classic Negroni cocktails also help turn the South Pacific into the south of France. A thoroughly unpretentious affair, it's worth a stop before or after dining along Ponsonby Rd. (www.annabelswinebar.com; 277 Ponsonby Rd; 3-11pm)

Satya Chai Lounge
BAR

18 MAP P86, G5

Craft beers – many from Wellington's iconic Garage Project brewery – partner with fiery

Indian street food in this rustic and laid-back space. Cocktails and a well-considered wine list complete the picture. There's no signage, so be brave and push the door open to the cosy interior. Next door with a great whisky selection is the equally hip tiki-inspired GGX Flamingo bar. (09-377 0007; www.satya.co.nz/satya-chai-lounge; 271 Karangahape Rd; noon-1.30pm & 6-10pm)

Wine Cellar   WINE BAR

Secreted downstairs in an arcade, the Wine Cellar (see 21, Map p86, H5) is dark, grungy and very cool, with regular live music in the neighbouring Whammy Bar. (www.facebook.com/winecellarstkevins; St Kevin's Arcade, 183 Karangahape Rd; 5pm-midnight Mon-Thu, to 1am Fri & Sat)

Brewers Co-operative   CRAFT BEER

19   MAP P86, H1

With 27 craft beers on tap, this corner bar is a good central-city option for an interesting brew and a feed of seafood and chips served the traditional way, in paper. It's popular with the after-work crowd on Fridays. (09-309 4515; 128 Victoria St; 11am-10pm)

Entertainment

Whammy Bar   LIVE MUSIC

It's small, but this bar (see 21, Map p86, H5) is a stalwart on the live indie-music scene nonetheless. (www.facebook.com/thewhammybar; 183 Karangahape Rd; 8.30pm-4am Wed-Sat)

Hoppers Garden Bar

St Kevin's Arcade

Neck of the Woods
LIVE MUSIC

20 MAP P86, H5

New Zealand's best indie bands, emerging overseas acts, drum-and-bass DJs and the occasional burlesque show all feature at this versatile upstairs venue keeping the creative spirit of Karangahape Rd alive. (09-320 5221; www.neckofthewoods.co.nz; 155 Karangahape Rd; varies by event)

Shopping

St Kevin's Arcade
SHOPPING CENTRE

21 MAP P86, H5

Built in 1924, this historic, renovated shopping arcade has interesting stores selling vintage clothing and organic and sustainable goods. The arcade also has excellent cafes and restaurants. (www.stkevinsarcade.co.nz; 183 Karangahape Rd)

Cross Street Market
MARKET

22 MAP P86, H5

Vintage apparel, art and design from NZ craftspeople and good coffee make this raffish market a highlight of exploring Karangahape Rd's bohemian scene. (4 Cross St; 10am-5pm)

Crushes
ARTS & CRAFTS

23 MAP P86, H5

Sells an excellent selection of arts, crafts, foodstuffs and homewares from local NZ designers. Also an interesting array of vintage clothing. (📞09-940 5065; www.crushes.co.nz; 225 Karangahape Rd; ⓘ10am-6pm Mon-Fri, to 5pm Sat, 11am-5pm Sun)

Zambesi CLOTHING

24 MAP P86, C4

Designed by Liz and Neville Findlay, the iconic Zambesi label offers sought-after NZ clothing coveted by both locals and internationals. (📞09-360 7391; www.zambesi.co.nz; 169 Ponsonby Rd; ⓘ10am-6pm Mon-Fri, 11am-5pm Sat & Sun)

Women's Bookshop BOOKS

25 MAP P86, C4

Excellent independent bookshop with a great selection of NZ authors and NZ-themed books. (📞09-376 4399; www.womensbookshop.co.nz; 105 Ponsonby Rd; ⓘ10am-6pm Mon-Fri, to 5pm Sat & Sun)

Flying Out MUSIC

26 MAP P86, H5

Interesting vinyl aplenty overflows at this compact record shop, which is also a top place to pick up recordings from NZ musicians. Cool T-shirts make it worth a stop even if you're more into streaming. (📞09-366 1755; www.flyingout.co.nz; 80 Pitt St; ⓘ10am-6pm Mon-Thu, to 7pm Fri, to 5pm Sat & Sun)

Karen Walker CLOTHING

27 MAP P86, D5

Join Madonna and Kirsten Dunst in wearing Walker's cool (but pricey) threads. (📞09-361 6723; www.karenwalker.com; 128a Ponsonby Rd; ⓘ10am-5.30pm Mon-Sat, 11am-4pm Sun)

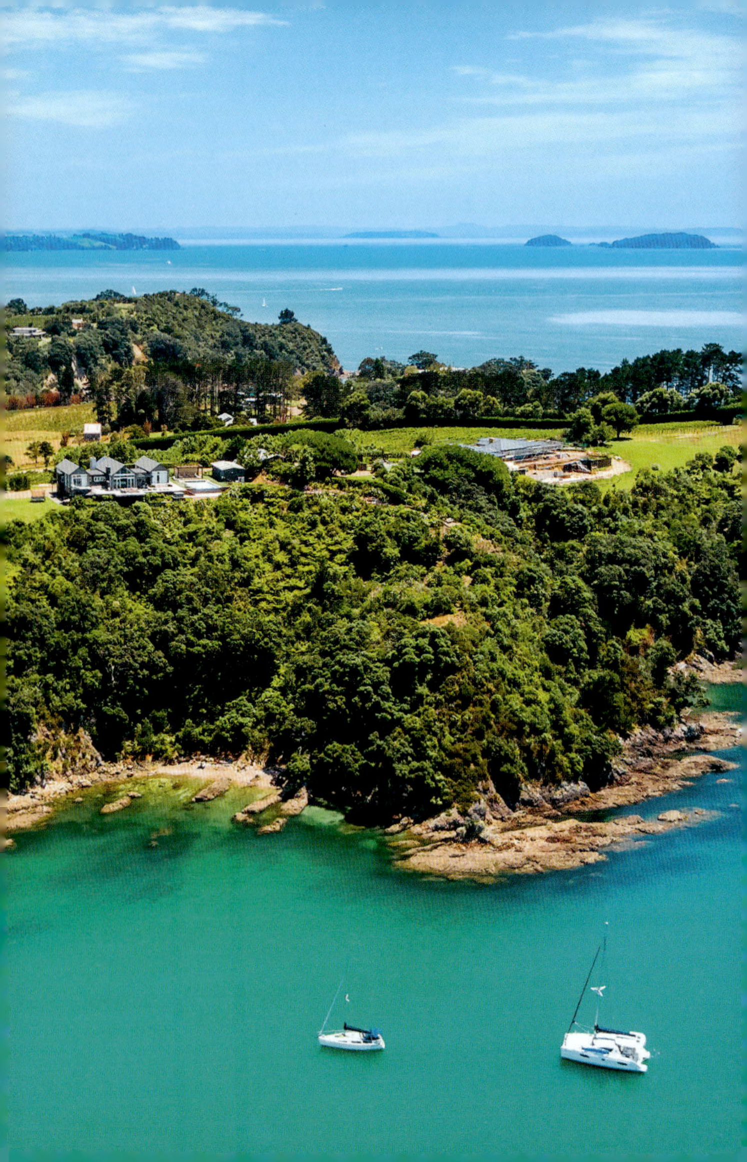

Explore
Waiheke Island

With a warm, dry microclimate, Waiheke Island is a favourite escape for city dwellers and visitors alike. Emerald waters lap at rocky bays and sandy beaches, while the island's vineyards combine tasting rooms, excellent restaurants and superb views. Art galleries are popular destinations, and for active travellers there's kayaking, zip lining and walking trails. All a short ferry ride from Auckland.

The Short List

- **Man O' War (p101)** Arriving by seaplane to this isolated beach with an excellent vineyard.
- **EcoZip Adventures (p101)** Soaring above native bush with vineyard and city views on this island zip line.
- **Tantalus Estate (p102)** Dining in a classy vineyard restaurant with the added attraction of excellent craft beers.
- **Potiki Adventures (p101)** Learning about the island from a Māori cultural perspective.
- **Three Seven Two (p102)** Relaxing at this waterfront destination-dining restaurant right on Onetangi Beach.

Getting There & Around

Fullers runs a passenger ferry from central Auckland, while Sealink operates vehicular ferries from central Auckland and Half Moon Bay in east Auckland.

Auckland Seaplanes flies from central Auckland.

Services include regular Auckland Transport buses and the hop-on, hop-off Waiheke Island Explorer service from Fullers.

Waiheke Island Map on p100

Driving Tour

Self-Drive Waiheke

Waiheke is a surprisingly large island, and renting a car is recommended to experience the best of it. Highlights include quiet beaches on the the island's more isolated eastern end, excellent coastal views towards the Coromandel Peninsula, and the opportunity to zip line above a vineyard. Along the way, expect plenty of opportunities for good eating and drinking.

Drive Facts

Start/End Matiatia ferry wharf

Length 54km; three to four hours

❶ Oneroa

Pick up your rental car from the passenger-ferry wharf at Matiatia and make the short drive to Oneroa village. Good shopping includes excellent galleries and craft shops, and the **Waiheke Wine Centre** (p103) has an extensive selection of the island's wines.

❷ Onetangi Rd

From Oneroa, drive 7km to the cluster of vineyards and restaurants on Onetangi Rd. Options include archery and laser clay shooting at **Wild on Waiheke** (p101) or wine tasting amid the southern European ambience of **Stonyridge** (p101). Nearby, **Tantalus Estate** (p102) also makes craft beer on site under the Alibi Brewing Company label.

❸ EcoZip Adventures

A short 3km drive away on winding roads is **EcoZip Adventures** (p101). Three separate zip lines – each around 200m long – provide island thrills, and there are excellent views of vineyards and the city as you're whizzing along.

❹ Onetangi Beach

The best beach on Waiheke's northern shore, Onetangi is a sweeping arc of sand that's good for swimming. Take extra care if the (usually gentle) waves are more boisterous. Options to relax, refuel and recharge include the excellent **Three Seven Two** (p102).

❺ Man O' War Bay

Yes, the 14km drive from Onetangi to Man O' War Bay on unsealed roads can be bumpy, but it is one of Waiheke's most beautiful spots. The sheltered beach is safe for swimming and a slender wooden wharf stretches into the water. An essential experience is the beachfront tasting room at **Man O' War** (p101) vineyard.

❻ Connells Bay

From Man O' War Bay, it's a further 6km on unsealed roads to **Connells Bay** (09-372 8957; www.connellsbay.co.nz; 142 Cowes Bay Rd; adult/child $30/15; by appointment late Oct–mid-Apr) where a private sculpture park features a stellar roster of NZ artists. Admission is only possible on a two-hour guided tour. Enquire about dates and book ahead online.

❼ Ostend

On the 21km drive back west to Oneroa, stop after 17km in Ostend, for Waiheke's best homestyle baking at **Island Coffee** (p103).

❽ Oneroa

From Ostend it's a 4km hop back to Oneroa – you've still got time for an ice cream at **Island Gelato** (p102) – before the short drive downhill to the ferry.

Waiheke Island

For reviews see
- Sights p101
- Eating p102
- Drinking p103
- Shopping p103

Sights

Man O' War WINERY

1 MAP P100, E2

Settle in with a tapas platter and a glass of Man O' War's Valhalla chardonnay at Waiheke's only beachfront tasting room. If the weather is good, go for a swim in beautiful Man O' War Bay. Options to reach the bay include private vehicle, a short but spectacular flight with Auckland Seaplanes (p53), or by prior reservation on Man O' War's summer-only bus from the **Matiatia Wharf**. See www.manowar.co.nz/book-a-bus. (09-372 9678; www.manowar.co.nz; 725 Man O' War Bay Rd; 11am-4pm Thu-Mon)

Stonyridge WINERY

2 MAP P100, C3

Waiheke's most famous vineyard is home to world-famous reds, an atmospheric cafe and the occasional yoga session on the breezy decks. Order a bottle of wine and a gigantic deli platter, and retreat to one of the cabanas in the garden. (09-372 8822; www.stonyridge.com; 80 Onetangi Rd; tastings per wine $10-18; 11.30am-5pm)

Wild on Waiheke WINERY

3 MAP P100, C3

Showcasing its offerings in a modern bar-and-bistro complex, this winery and microbrewery offers tastings and activities including archery and laser clay shooting. Kids can explore the cool wooden-castle playground while parents enjoy a few end-of-week drinks in the garden bar. Good food includes shared plates, mains and platters. (bookings for current week 09-372 3434, future & group bookings 09-372 4225; www.wildonwaiheke.co.nz; 82 Onetangi Rd; tastings per beer or wine $3; 11am-5pm Sat-Thu, to 9pm Fri;)

EcoZip Adventures ADVENTURE SPORTS

4 MAP P100, C3

With vineyard, native bush and ocean views, EcoZip's three separate 200m zip lines make for an exciting ride, and there's a gentle 1.5km walk back up through the bush after the thrills. Costs include free transfers from Matiatia Wharf or Oneroa if you don't have your own transport. Booking ahead online is essential. (09-372 5646; www.ecozipadventures.co.nz; 150 Trig Hill Rd; adult/child/family $129/79/337; 10.15am, 12.15pm & 2.15pm)

Potiki Adventures CULTURAL

Day-long island tours from a Māori cultural perspective, including beaches, a bushwalk, a vineyard visit, and demonstrations of traditional musical instruments and weaving. (021 422 773; www.potikiadventures.co.nz; adult/child $150/80)

Eating

Tantalus Estate — MODERN NZ $$$

5 MAP P100, C3

Up a winding driveway framed by grapevines, Waiheke's newest vineyard restaurant and tasting room channels an Iberian ambience, but the savvy and diverse menu effortlessly covers the globe. Secure a spot under rustic chandeliers crafted from repurposed tree branches, and enjoy a leisurely lunch imbued with Asian and Mediterranean influences. (09-372 2625; www.tantalus.co.nz; 70-72 Onetangi Rd; mains $38-44; 11am-5pm)

Three Seven Two — BISTRO $$$

6 MAP P100, C2

Referencing the first three digits of Waiheke phone numbers, Three Seven Two's oceanfront location includes an outdoor deck and a shaded rear courtyard. Local ingredients are harnessed for seasonal shared plates including shiitake mushroom dumplings, and bigger main dishes of Wagyu hanger steaks or an eggplant and chermoula pilaf. The drinks list includes local beer and wine. (www.threeseventwo.co.nz; 21 The Strand; shared plates $12-22, mains $34-39)

Casita Miro — SPANISH $$

7 MAP P100, C2

A wrought-iron-and-glass pavilion backed with a Gaudí-esque mosaic garden is the stage for a very entertaining troupe of servers who will guide you through the menu of delectable tapas and *raciones* (larger dishes), designed to be shared. In summer the sides open up, but otherwise, at busy times, it can get noisy. Book ahead. (09-372 7854; www.casitamiro.co.nz; 3 Brown Rd; tapas $9-19, ración $36-38; 11.30am-4pm Sun-Thu, to 8pm Fri & Sat)

Island Gelato — ICE CREAM $

8 MAP P100, A2

Before school, after school, and during weekdays and weekends, Waiheke locals crowd Island Gelato's shipping-container garden for delicious gelato, coffee and bagels. Seasonal gelato flavours shine, including our favourite, the zingy kaffir-lime-and-coconut sorbet. You'll find all this irresistible goodness at the bottom end of Oneroa village. (021 536 860; www.islandgelato.co.nz; 124 Oceanview Rd; ice cream from $6; 8am-7pm)

Dragonfired — PIZZA $

9 MAP P100, B2

Specialising in 'artisan wood-fired food', this caravan by the beach serves the three Ps: pizza, polenta plates and pocket bread. It's one of Waiheke's best places for cheap eats. (021 922 289; www.dragonfired.co.nz; Little Oneroa Beach; mains $12-16; 10am-8pm daily Nov-Mar, 11am-7pm Fri-Sun Apr-Oct;)

Vineyard, Waiheke Island

Drinking

Island Coffee CAFE

10 MAP P100, B3

Search out this bohemian spot for Waiheke's best coffee – served with delicious homestyle baking (try the cinnamon brioche) – and the chance to spin some retro tunes from the selection of vintage vinyl. It's a compact spot, so be prepared to grab a takeaway coffee. (www.islandcoffeenz.com; 21b Belgium St; 8.30am-12.30pm Tue-Sat)

Shopping

Waiheke Wine Centre WINE

11 MAP P100, A2

Located in Oneroa's main street, this well-stocked and authoritative store features wine from all of Waiheke's vineyards, and is a good place to pick up information on wine destinations around the island. A special sampling system allows customers to purchase pours of various wines. (09-372 6139; www.waihekewinecentre.com; 153 Oceanview Rd; 9.30am-7.30pm Mon-Thu, to 8pm Fri & Sat, from 10am Sun)

Worth a Trip
Great Barrier Island

The most rugged and remote of the islands in Auckland's Hauraki Gulf, Great Barrier Island has traditionally been appreciated for its unspoiled beaches, hiking tracks and lush native bush. Now the Barrier's isolation is also making it one of the southern hemisphere's best locations to observe the night sky. It was designated a Dark Sky Sanctuary in 2017 and, for visitors from the northern hemisphere, it offers a unique opportunity.

★ Getting There
Most visitors fly to Great Barrier Island from Auckland in just 30 minutes, but it can also be reached on a Sealink car ferry (four to five hours) from central Auckland.

Exploring the Island

Book with local operators who really know the island to make the most of a visit.

Paddles & Saddles (📞027 410 2688; www.paddlesandsaddles.co.nz; 207 Puriri Bay Rd; scooter per day $59, single/double/fishing kayak per half-day $50/65/65) is an excellent rental spot run by the friendly Lucy and Pete with options including scooters, kayaks and paddle boards. Fishing and snorkelling gear is available, and there's simple but good-value shared-bathroom accommodation at their idyllic harbourfront location (double $95 to $120). Don't miss taking a moonlit dip in the outdoor bathtubs.

Contact **Hooked on Barrier** (📞09-429 0740; www.hookedonbarrier.co.nz; Claris; casual fishing trip per person $130, half-/full-day boat charter $850/1600) for fishing and diving charters and sightseeing tours. Sightseeing cruises including lunch or dinner are $150 to $165 per person.

Crazy Horse Trike Tours (📞0800 997 222, 📞09-429 0222; www.greatbarrierislandtourism.co.nz; per person from $75) offers entertaining trips around the island. Options include two-hour sightseeing tours, beach visits, kayaking, hot springs and forest walks. Owner Steve Billingham is a very entertaining source of information on interesting local stories and island history.

Star Treks (📞021 865 836; https://startreks.kiwi; 2 people from $395) provides excellent walking experiences, combining local history, flora, scenery and dark-sky viewing. Walks are often led by co-operator Benny Bellerby, born and bred on the island, with organic and sustainably sourced snacks and drinks provided for refreshment.

Hiking

The island's popular walking tracks are outlined in the Department of Conservation's free *Great Barrier Island (Aotea Island)* booklet. Make sure you're properly equipped with water and food, and be prepared for both sunny and wet weather.

★ Top Tips

○ Book a package incorporating car hire, flights and accommodation with **Go Great Barrier Island** (📞0800 997 222; www.greatbarrierislandtourism.co.nz).

○ Book a few nights on the island as weather conditions may not be suitable for dark-sky viewing when you first arrive.

✕ Take a Break

Big breakfasts and salads combine with good coffee and outdoor seating at **My Fat Puku** (📞09-429 0811; www.facebook.com/myfatpuku; 129 Hector Sanderson Rd; mains $15-23; ⏰8am-4pm; 🍴). Menu highlights include the Puku burrito with chicken and chilli jam for a Barrier brunch. From late December to Easter, opening hours are extended and it's time for cold beers, wood-fired pizza and cocktails made from the Barrier's very own Island Gin.

The most popular easy walk is the 45-minute **Kaitoke Hot Springs Track**, starting from Whangaparapara Rd and leading to natural hot springs in a bush stream. Check the temperature before getting in and don't put your head under the water.

Windy Canyon Lookout, which is only a 15-minute walk from Aotea Rd, has spectacular rock outcrops and affords great views of the island.

Beaches

The beaches on the west coast are safe, but care needs to be taken on the surf-pounded eastern beaches. **Medlands Beach** is one of the most beautiful and accessible beaches on the island. Remote **Whangapoua**, in the northeast, requires more effort to get to, while **Kaitoke**, **Awana Bay** and **Harataonga** on the east coast are also worth a visit.

Okiwi Bar has an excellent right-hand break, while Awana has both left- and right-hand breaks. Diving is excellent, with shipwrecks, pinnacles, lots of fish and more than 33m visibility at some times of the year.

Going Green on Great Barrier

Although only 88km from Auckland, Great Barrier is a world away, and the island's resilient and creative residents are avid proponents of sustainable off-the-grid living. Electricity is mainly generated by private solar and wind setups, and a few local businesses are making this their unique point of difference.

Visit **Aotea Brewing** (www.aoteabrewing.co.nz; 50a Mason Rd; ⏲noon-6pm Fri-Sun) to purchase craft beers brewed off the grid in the compact on-site microbrewery. Beers including Solar American Pale Ale are available in sustainable and recyclable bottles, both at Aotea's rustic taproom, and at the Rocks bottle shop in Claris.

Crafted entirely off the grid and harnessing local forest botanicals, Island Gin is also available at the Rocks and at the excellent **Currach Irish Pub** (📞09-429 0211; www.currachirishpub.co.nz; 78 Blackwell Dr; mains $20-34; ⏲4pm-late Boxing Day-Easter, closed Wed Mar-Dec; 📶♿) in Tryphena.

For a more sustainable alternative to a car or 4WD – and to combat the island's high fuel prices – **Motubikes** (📞022 344 0645; www.motubikes.co.nz; 67 Hector Sanderson Rd; per hour/day $25/90; ⏲10am-4pm) rents out sturdy electric motorcycles equally at home on unsealed roads. The chatty owner can arrange drop-off and pick-up services around the island.

Experiencing the Night Sky

With no mains power or street lights here, light pollution is minimal. The Milky Way, constellations and other celestial attractions – sometimes including Saturn and Jupiter – can be seen through telescopes and with the naked eye, and Dark Sky Ambassadors from **Good Heavens** (📞09-429 0876; www.goodheavens.co.nz; group tours per person $120, minimum 2 people private tours $600) can even set up their sky-watching gear at your accommodation. Booking ahead is vital, preferably for your first night on the island in case the weather is less than ideal.

0 4 km
0 2 miles
Needles Point
Aiguilles Island
Great Barrier Forest
Tataweka (526m)
Miners Head
Rangiwhakaea Bay
SOUTH PACIFIC OCEAN
Motairehe Stm
Ahuriri Point
Waikaro Point
Katherine Bay
Motairehe
Maunganui Point
Kawa
Whangapoua Beach
Rakitu Island
Whangapoua Creek
Orama
Motuhaku Island
Tree Peak (210m)
Okiwi
Port FitzRoy
Coopers Castle (465m)
Whangawahia (361m)
Harataonga Bay
Whakatautuna Point
Kaikoura Island
Kaiaraara Bay
Hirakimata (Mt Hobson) (621m)
Mt Heale (510m)
Korotiti Bay
Opakau Island
Port Fitzroy
Mt Young (372m)
Mt Matawhero (425m)
Awana Bay
Maungapiko (280m)
Kaitoke Hot Springs
Kauri Falls
Mt Whangaparapara (309m)
My Fat Puku
Kaitoke Beach
Junction Islands
Whangaparapara
Claris
Pitokuku Island
Wairahi Forest Sanctuary
Te Ahumata (394m)
Hooked on Barrier
Okupu
Oruawharo Bay
Aotea Brewing
Blind Bay
Medlands Beach
St Paul (401m)
Tryphena
Paddles & Saddles
Curraeh Irish Pub
Shag Point
Tryphena Harbour
Hauraki Gulf
Ferry to Auckland
Cape Barrier

Top Sight 📷
Tamaki Drive

Hugging the waterfront, this scenic pohutukawa-lined road heads east from the city, and is popular for running, cycling and rollerblading. Peaceful swimming beaches start at Okahu Bay, and around the headland is Mission Bay with its good cafes, restaurants, and a heritage art-deco fountain. More safe swimming beaches and more good eating also feature at Kohimarama and St Heliers.

★ Getting There

Catch the bright-blue TāmakiLink bus from the Britomart Transport Centre (adult/child $5.50/3) towards St Heliers. The service includes stops at Okahu Bay, Mission Bay, Kohimarama and St Heliers.

Kelly Tarlton's Sea Life Aquarium

At **Kelly Tarlton's** (09-531 5065; www.kellytarltons.co.nz; 23 Tamaki Dr; adult/child $39/27; 9.30am-5pm) topsy-turvy aquarium, sharks and stingrays swim over and around you in transparent tunnels that were once stormwater tanks. You can also enter the tanks in a shark cage with a snorkel ($89). Other attractions include the Penguin Passport tour (10.30am Tuesday, Thursday and Saturday, $179 per person), where visitors can get up close with Antarctic penguins. For all tickets, there are significant discounts online, especially for midweek visits.

Kayaking from Tamaki Drive

Tamaki Dr is a popular departure point for kayaking trips on Auckland harbour. Contact **Auckland Sea Kayaks** (0800 999 089; www.aucklandseakayaks.co.nz; 384 Tamaki Dr) for guided trips (including lunch) to Rangitoto Island ($195, 6½ hours) and Motukorea (Browns Island; $155, four hours). Multiday excursions and sunset paddles are also available. Located just west of Okahu Bay, **Fergs Kayaks** (09-529 2230; www.fergskayaks.co.nz; 12 Tamaki Dr; 9am-5pm) offers guided kayak trips across the harbour to Devonport ($100, three hours, 8km), or across to Rangitoto Island ($160, six hours, 13km). Fergs can also hook up travellers with kayaks (per hour from $25), paddle boards ($30), bikes ($20) and inline skates ($20). After all that honest exercise, adjourn to the **Good George Craft House** (09-974 0006; www.goodgeorgemissionbay.co.nz; 71 Tamaki Dr; 11.30am-midnight) in Mission Bay for a refreshing craft beer.

★ Top Tips

- Achilles Bay Lookout is the ideal vantage point for gazing over Auckland Harbour and the Hauraki Gulf. Traditional Māori carvings honour important historical chiefs.

- A free shark-shaped shuttle bus to Kelly Tarlton's Sea Life Aquarium departs from near Britomart Transport Centre hourly from 9.30am to 3.30pm.

✕ Take a Break

At the eastern end of Tamaki Dr, **St Heliers Bay Bistro** (www.stheliersbaybistro.co.nz; 387 Tamaki Dr; brunch $16-27, dinner $27-34; 7am-11pm) is a classy eatery with harbour views. Look forward to upmarket takes on the classics (pasta, burgers, fish and chips), along with cooked breakfasts, tasty salads and lots of Mediterranean influences. Excellent ice cream as well.

Worth a Trip
West Auckland

The West Auckland region epitomises rugged black-sand beaches, bush-shrouded ranges and surf rolling in from the Tasman Sea. Add to the mix Croatian immigrants, earning the fertile fields under the Waitākere Ranges the nickname 'Dallie Valley', after the Dalmatian coast where most hailed from. These pioneering families planted grapes and made wine, founding one of New Zealand's major industries.

★ Getting There

The highlights of West Auckland are difficult to reach by public transport. Consider renting a car or joining a tour focused on the area's vineyards or surf beaches.

Titirangi

This leafy village marks the end of Auckland's suburban sprawl and is a good place for a coffee or breakfast stop en route to the west-coast beaches. Located amid the heritage vibe of Lopdell House, **Deco Eatery** (09-817 2664; www.decoeatery.co.nz; Lopdell House, 418 Titirangi Rd; mains $16-38; 7am-late Mon-Fri, 7.30am-late Sat & Sun;) channels a Turkish ambience, while the menu combines Anatolian classics with a broader Mediterranean focus. Lopdell House also hosts the excellent **Te Uru Waitakere Contemporary Gallery** (09-817 8087; www.teuru.org.nz; 420 Titirangi Rd; admission free; 10am-4.30pm). New Zealand's greatest modern painter, Colin McCahon used to live in Titirangi in the 1950s, and his former cottage and studio is now open as **McCahon House** (09-817 6148; www.facebook.com/McCahonHouse; 67 Otitori Bay Rd; $5; 1-4pm Wed-Sun), a compact museum dedicated to his life and work.

Piha

The most famous of Auckland's surf-battered, black-sand, west-coast beaches, Piha (pictured left) is perfect for surfing, rough-and-tumble swimming (between the flags only – it's one of the region's most dangerous beaches) and moody, wintry walks. The offshore drama is echoed by a magnificently rugged landscape dominated by large rock outcrops and imposing cliffs. Perched majestically on the sands, **Lion Rock** is an imposing outcrop that dominates the southern end of the beach. It's all that's left of an ancient volcano after many millennia of being lashed by the ocean.

Muriwai

A rugged black-sand surf beach, Muriwai Beach's main claim to fame is the **Takapu Refuge gannet colony**, spread over the

★ Top Tips

○ Specialist tour companies exploring the West Auckland wine region include **Auckland Wine Trail Tours** (09-630 1540; www.winetrail tours.co.nz) and **Fine Wine Tours** (0800 023 111; www.insider touring.co.nz).

○ To explore west coast beaches including Piha and Muriwai, contact **TIME Unlimited** (09-846 3469; www.newzealandtours.travel; adult/child from $295/147.50) or **Bush & Beach** (09-837 4130; www.bushandbeach.co.nz).

✕ Take a Break

It's not only wine making waves in West Auckland. Hallertau (p115) offers tasting paddles ($12 to $16) of its craft beers served in its spacious and sociable *biergarten*, and inside on cosy tables near the bar.

southern headland and outlying rock stacks. Viewing platforms get you close enough to watch (and smell) these fascinating seabirds. Every August hundreds of adult birds return to this spot to hook up with their regular partners and get busy – expect lots of outrageously cute neck rubbing, bill touching and general snuggling. The net result is a single chick per season; December and January are the best times to see the little ones testing their wings before embarking on an impressive odyssey.

Nearby, a couple of short tracks will take you through beautiful native bush to a lookout that offers views along the 60km length of the beach.

The Great Gannet OE

After honing their flying skills, young gannets get the ultimate chance to test them – a 2000km journey to Australia. They usually hang out there for several years before returning home, never to attempt the journey again. Once back in the homeland they spend a few years waiting for a piece of waterfront property to become available in the colony, before settling down with a regular partner to nest – returning to the same patch of dirt every year. In other words, they're your typical young New Zealander on their rite-of-passage Overseas Experience (OE).

Welcome to Wine Country

Located around the rapidly growing rural town of Kumeū, West Auckland's main wine-producing area still has some vineyards owned by the original Croatian families who kick-started NZ's wine industry. The fancy eateries that have mushroomed in recent years have done little to dent the relaxed farmland feel to the region, but done everything to encourage an afternoon's indulgence on the way back from the beaches or the **Parakai Springs** (09-420 8998; www.parakaisprings.co.nz; 150 Parkhurst Rd; adult/child $26/13; 10am-8pm Sun-Thu, to 9pm Fri & Sat;) hot pools in nearby Helensville. Most cellars offer free tastings.

Where to Drink

Recommended wineries include **Coopers Creek** (09-412 8560; www.cooperscreek.co.nz; 601 SH16; 10.30am-5.30pm), where you can buy a bottle and spread out for a picnic in the attractive gardens. From January to Easter, the vineyard hosts Sunday afternoon jazz sessions. Owned by the Brajkovich family, **Kumeu River** (09-412 8415; www.kumeuriver.co.nz; 550 SH16; 9am-4.30pm Mon-Fri, from 11am Sat & Sun) produces one of NZ's best chardonnays, among other varietals. One of the pioneering Croat-Kiwi family vineyards, **Soljans Estate** (09-412 5858; www.soljans.co.nz; 366 SH16; tastings 9am-5pm, cafe to 3pm) has a wonderful cafe offering good-value brunch and lunch set menus

Parakai Springs
Parakai
Helensville
Te Pua
Kaipara River
16
Woodhill
Woodhill Forest
Dairy Flat
1
Rangitopuni Stream
Coatesville
Albany
Riverhead
Hallertau
Tasting Shed
Huapai
Kumeu River
Waimauku
Kumeū
Coopers Creek
Beer Spot
Soljans Estate
18
Waitematā Harbour
Muriwai Beach
Waitākere
Swanson
16
Auckland
Bethells Cafe
Te Henga (Bethells Beach)
Te Uru Waitakere Contemporary Gallery
New Lynn
Deco Eatery
Waiatarua
Scenic Dr
Titirangi
McCahon House
Piha
Waitākere Ranges Regional Park
Laingholm
Tasman Sea
Karekare
Huia
Manukau Harbour
Cornwallis
Little Huia
Whatipu
0 4 km
0 2 miles

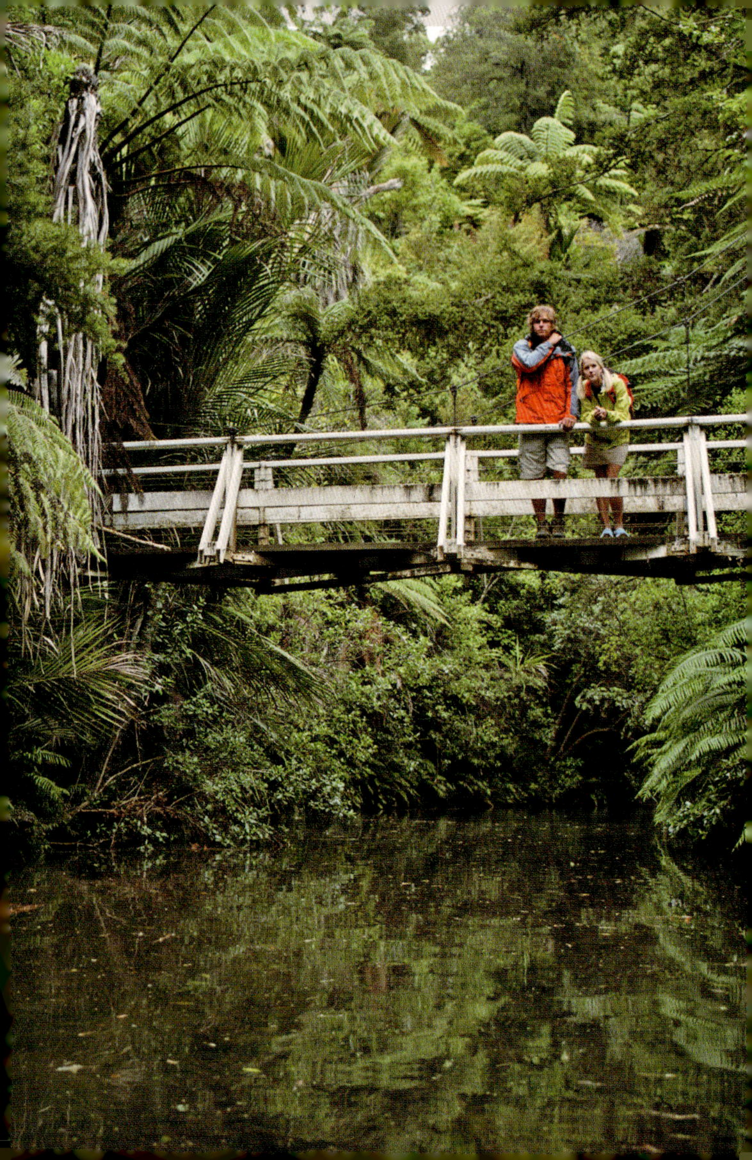

and buffets. For a hoppy haven in wine country, head to the **Beer Spot** (☏09-974 1496; www.thebeerspot.co.nz; 321 Main Rd; ⏱noon-8pm Mon & Tue, to 9pm Wed, to 10pm Thu-Sun) in nearby Huapai.

Where to Eat

With good wine and beer, good eating naturally follows, and a vibrant restaurant scene is enlivening the area's traditionally rural vibe. Dining options include excellent food at **Hallertau** (☏09-412 5555; www.hallertau.co.nz; 1171 Coatesville-Riverhead Hwy; sharing plates $11-24, mains $25-35; ⏱11am-10pm). and the **Tasting Shed** (☏09-412 6454; www.thetastingshed.co.nz; 609 SH16; dishes $16-32; ⏱4-10pm Wed & Thu, noon-11pm Fri-Sun; 🍴) is a slick eatery with dishes inspired by the flavours of Asia, the Middle East and Mediterranean Europe.

Waitākere Ranges

This 160-sq-km wilderness (pictured left) was covered in kauri until the mid-19th century, when logging claimed most of the giant trees. A few stands of ancient kauri and other mature natives survive amid the dense bush of the regenerating rainforest, which is now protected inside the Waitākere Ranges Regional Park. Bushwalking in the park is popular, but has been limited in recent years because of the kauri dieback disease damaging the park's forests. Search for 'track closures' on www.aucklandcouncil.govt.nz for the latest information before setting off.

Bay of Islands Regions

Russell (p129)
Connected by ferry to Paihia but a world away, historic Russell is close to beautiful beaches, wineries and sailing adventures. Stroll the waterfront by the striking pohutukawa trees.

Paihia (p119)
Activity, accommodation and restaurant centre of the Bay of Islands. Plus cycling, hiking, and the Waitangi Treaty Grounds nearby.

Kerikeri (p137)
Thriving Kerikeri is the fertile foodie hub of the region with a strong community of artisans. Its riverside mission and Kororipo Pā are a must-see.

Explore the Bay of Islands

For many New Zealanders, the phrase 'up north' evokes sepia-toned images of family holidays with red pohutukawa in bloom and dolphins frolicking in turquoise bays. Beaches are the main draw, from sheltered inlets to surf spots. Visitors from more crowded countries may be flummoxed to wander onto a sandy strip without a scrap of development or another human in sight.

It's not just natural attractions that are on offer in Northland: this is also the birthplace of modern New Zealand with the earliest settlements of both Māori and Europeans and its most significant site, the Waitangi Treaty Grounds.

Paihia **119**

Russell **129**

Kerikeri **137**

Top Sight
Waitangi Treaty Grounds 120

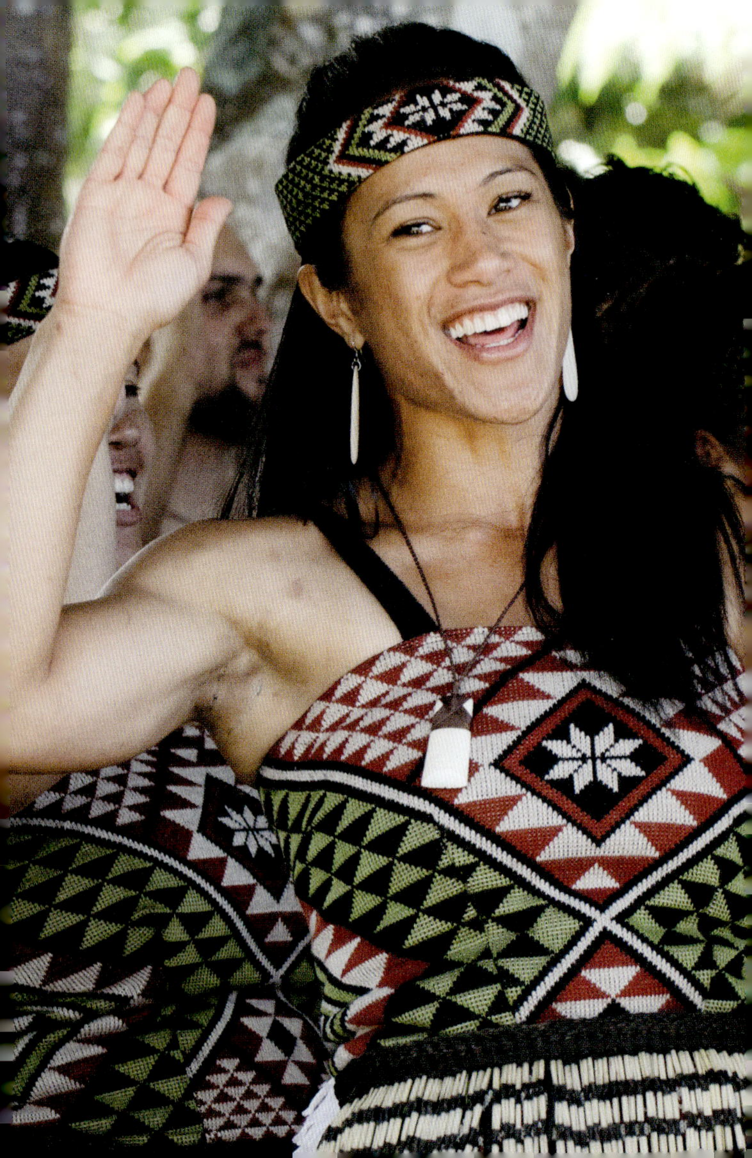

Explore
Paihia

Paihia is a gentle tourism-focused town, with an abundance of accommodation and good restaurants, plenty of tours as well as DIY options to get you out on the water, and a strong community spirit that lifts the vibe a few notches. Just to its north, Waitangi inhabits a special but somewhat complex place in the national psyche.

The Short List

- **Waitangi Treaty Grounds (p120)** *Getting to grips with the birth of New Zealand, not Aotearoa.*
- **Taiamai Tours Heritage Journeys (p123)** *Heading for the falls in a waka (canoe).*
- **Kayaking (p123)** *Hiring some kayaks at the beach and getting out on the water.*
- **Zane Grey's (p126)** *Drinking sundowners over the water never tasted so good.*
- **Flying Fish (p127)** *Buying yourself or someone you love a beautiful Kiwi gift.*

Getting There & Around

🚌 Buses serving Paihia stop at the Maritime Building by the wharf. Three to four coaches a day head to and from Auckland.

⛴ Regular departures to Russell. The car ferry to Russell leaves from nearby Opua.

Paihia Map on p122

Māori dance performance, Waitangi (p120) CHAMELEONSEYE/SHUTTERSTOCK ©

Top Sight 📷
Waitangi Treaty Grounds

Occupying a headland draped in lawns and bush, this is NZ's most significant historic site. Here, on 6 February 1840, after much discussion, the first 43 Māori chiefs signed the Treaty of Waitangi with the British Crown; eventually, over 500 chiefs would sign it. Admission includes entry to the Museum of Waitangi, the Whare Rūnanga (Carved Meeting House) and the historic Treaty House.

◎ MAP P122, A1
☏ 09-402 7437
www.waitangi.org.nz
1 Tau Henare Dr
adult/child $50/free
⊙ 9am-5pm

Te Kōngahu Museum of Waitangi

Opened in 2016, Te Kōngahu Museum of Waitangi is a modern and comprehensive showcase of the role of the treaty in the past, present and future of Aotearoa New Zealand. It provides a warts-and-all look at the early interactions between Māori and Europeans, the events leading up to the treaty's signing, the long litany of treaty breaches by the Crown, the wars and land confiscations that followed, and the protest movement that led to the current process of redress for historic injustices.

Many *taonga* (treasures) associated with Waitangi were previously scattered around NZ, and this excellent museum is now a repository for a number of important historical items. One room is devoted to facsimiles of all the key documents, while another screens a fascinating short film dramatising the events of the initial treaty signing.

Treaty House

The Treaty House was shipped over as a kitset from Australia and erected in 1834 as the four-room home of the official British Resident James Busby. It's now preserved as a memorial and museum containing displays about the house and the people who lived here. Just across the lawn, the magnificently detailed Whare Rūnanga (Carved Meeting House) was completed in 1940 to mark the centenary of the treaty. The fine carvings represent the major Māori tribes. It's here that the cultural performances take place, starting with a *haka pōwhiri* (challenge and welcome) and then heading inside for *waiata* (songs) and spine-tingling *haka* (war dances).

★ Top Tips

○ Near the cove is the 35m, 6-tonne *waka taua* (war canoe) *Ngātokimatawhaorua*, built for the centenary.

○ Leave time for the excellent gift shop selling Māori art and design, with a carving studio attached.

✕ Take a Break

The popular Whare Waka Cafe (p125) is the spot to take a break and enjoy brunch or lunch in a treed garden, south of the main entry off the car park.

★ Getting There

It's a short 2km drive, walk or cycle from central Paihia over a single-lane bridge.

Paihia

Map

A1 Waitangi Treaty Grounds (Top Sight)

- 1 Taiamai Tours Heritage Journeys — A2
- 2 Flying Kiwi Parasail — D1 (enlargement)
- 3 Coastal Kayakers — B2
- 4 Explore NZ — C2 (enlargement)
- 5 Fullers Great Sights — D2 (enlargement)
- 6 (Sight) — A4
- 7 Opua Forest — C6
- 8 St Paul's Anglican Church — D4
- 9 Williams House & Gardens — C2 (enlargement)
- 10 Awesome NZ — D2 (enlargement)

Eating
- 11 (Eating) — C1 (enlargement)
- 12 (Eating) — D1 (enlargement)
- 13 (Eating) — A1
- 14 (Eating) — D5
- 15 (Eating) — C1 (enlargement)
- 16 (Eating) — B3

Shopping
- 17 (Shopping) — C2 (enlargement)

For reviews see
- 🔴 Top Sights — p120
- 🔴 Sights — p123
- ❎ Eating — p125
- 🅰 Shopping — p127

Kororareka Bay
Te Ti Bay
Motumaire Island
Opua Forest
Horotutu Scenic Reserve
Ferry to Russell

0 — 500 m / 0.25 miles

Sights

Taiamai Tours Heritage Journeys
CULTURAL

1 ◉ MAP P122, A2

Paddle a traditional 12m carved *waka* (canoe) from the Waitangi bridge to the Haruru Falls. The Ngāpuhi hosts wear traditional garb, perform the proper *karakia* (incantations) and share stories. The price includes admission to the Waitangi Treaty Grounds (p120) at your leisure (which is otherwise $50). (📞09-405 9990; www.taiamaitours.co.nz; 3hr tour $135; ⏱departs 9am Tue, Thu, Sat & Sun Oct-Apr)

R Tucker Thompson
BOATING

Run by a charitable trust with an education focus, the *Tucker* is a majestic tall ship offering day sails (adult/child $159/79.50, including a barbecue lunch) and late-afternoon cruises (adult/child $67/33.75). (📞09-402 8430; www.tucker.co.nz; ⏱Nov-Mar)

Flying Kiwi Parasail
PARASAILING

2 ◉ MAP P122, D1

Departs from both Paihia and Russell wharves for New Zealand's highest parasail (1200ft/366m). (📞09-402 6068; www.parasailnz.com; solo $129, tandem per adult/child $99/69)

Coastal Kayakers
KAYAKING

3 ◉ MAP P122, A2

Runs guided tours (half-/full day from $75 per person, minimum two people) and multiday adventures. Kayaks (half-/full day $20/25) can also be rented for independent exploration. (📞0800 334 661; www.coastalkayakers.co.nz; Te Karuwha Pde)

Explore NZ
CRUISE

4 ◉ MAP P122, C2

Explore's four-hour Discover the Bay cruise (adult/child $149/90 including barbecue lunch) heads to the Hole in the Rock and stops at Urupukapuka Island. (📞09-359 5987; www.exploregroup.co.nz; cnr Marsden & Williams Rds)

She's a Lady
BOATING

Day sails include lunch, fishing, snorkelling and paddling a see-through-bottomed kayak. (📞0800 724 584; www.sailingbayofislands.com; day sail $100)

Phantom
BOATING

A fast 15m racing sloop, known for its great platters. It has a licensed cash bar on board. (📞0800 224 421; www.phantomsailingbayofislands.com; day sail $125)

Fullers Great Sights
CRUISE

5 ◉ MAP P122, D2

The four-hour Hole in the Rock Cruise heads out to the famous sea arch and stops at Urupukapuka Island on the way back. Boats stop at Russell wharf for pickups on all trips. (☏09-402 7421; www.dolphincruises.co.nz; Maritime Bldg, Marsden Rd)

Haruru Falls
WATERFALL

6 ◎ MAP P122, A4

A walking track (one way 1½ hours, 5km) leads from the Treaty Grounds along the Waitangi River to these attractive horseshoe falls. Part of the path follows a boardwalk through the mangroves. Otherwise you can drive here, reaching Haruru Falls Rd by turning right of Puketona Rd. (Haruru Falls Rd)

Opua Forest
FOREST

7 ◎ MAP P122, C5

Just behind Paihia, this regenerating forest has walking trails ranging from 10 minutes to five hours. A few large trees have escaped axe and fire, including some big kauri. Information on Opua Forest walks is available from the **i-SITE** (☏09-402 7345; www.northlandnz.com; 35 Walton St; ⏲8:30am-5pm Mar-Dec, to 7pm Jan & Feb), including the 1.5km **Paihia School Road Track** (about 30 minutes each way) leading to a lookout. You can also drive into the forest by taking Oromahoe Rd west from Opua. (www.doc.govt.nz)

St Paul's Anglican Church
CHURCH

8 ◎ MAP P122, D4

The characterful St Paul's was constructed of Kawakawa stone in 1925, and stands on the site of the original mission church, a simple raupo (bulrush) hut erected in 1823. Look for the native birds in the stained glass above the altar – the kotare (kingfisher) represents Jesus, while the tui (parson bird) and kererū (wood pigeon) portray the personalities of the Williams brothers (one scholarly, one forceful), who set up the mission station here. (36 Marsden Rd)

Williams House & Gardens
HISTORIC BUILDING

9 ◎ MAP P122, C2

The historic buildings and gardens of Paihia's First Mission Station include a restored stone store, and now house a community library and a secondhand bookshop. Free public wi-fi is available here too. (www.williamshousepaihia.com; Williams Rd; admission free)

Haruru Falls

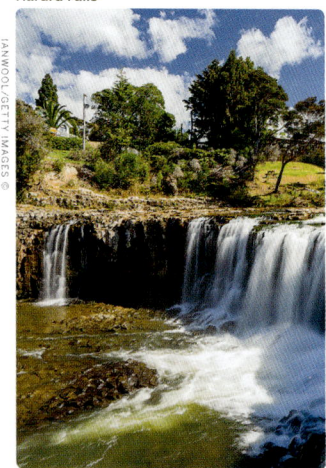

Awesome NZ
BUS

10 🎯 MAP P122, D2

Trips to Cape Reinga include sandboarding, a short walk in the Puketi Forest, and stops for a snack at Taipa and to devour fish and chips at Mangonui. (📞0800 486 877; www.awesomenz.com; Maritime Bldg, Marsden Rd; tour from $140)

Eating

Terra
SEAFOOD $$$

11 ❌ MAP P122, C1

Muted colours give way to sea views at this new upstairs seafood restaurant across from Paihia pier. The seasonal menu is largely seafood focused (who can resist Orongo Bay oysters with lemon, seaweed, horopito and sherry mignonette?), but promises to take care of fine-dining vegetarians on request. Be advised to leave room for the cheese-tasting menu with a mix of French and local cheese. (📞09-945 8376; info@terrarestaurant.co.nz; 76 Marsden Rd; mains $20-38; 🕔5.30pm-late Tue-Sun)

Charlotte's Kitchen
CONTEMPORARY $$

12 ❌ MAP P122, D1

Named after an escaped Australian convict who was NZ's first white female settler, this hip restaurant-bar occupies a cheeky perch on the main pier. Bits of Kiwiana decorate the walls, while the menu takes a swashbuckling journey around the world, including steamed pork

---

> ### Cycle from Coast to Coast 🚴
>
> The **Twin Coast Cycle Trail** (Pou Herenga Tai) stretches from the Bay of Islands right across the country to the Hokianga Harbour. It's only 87km, but it definitely gives you boasting rights when you get home. The complete route takes two days and travels from Opua to Kawakawa, Kaikohe, Okaihau and Horeke before finishing at Mangungu Mission Station.
>
> If you're cycling to Horeke, be aware that the pub there is only open to staying and paying customers; book ahead if you want a meal or a place to sleep.
>
> The trail is well described at www.twincoastcycletrail.kiwi.nz, where you'll find all the information on bike hire from various towns and shuttle transport to bring you back if you run out of puff.

---

buns, fresh oysters and pizzas. (📞09-402 8296; www.charlotteskitchen.co.nz; Paihia Wharf, 69 Marsden Rd; mains lunch $16-27, dinner $20-35; 🕔11.30am-10pm Mon-Fri, to 11pm Sat & Sun)

Whare Waka Cafe
CAFE $$

13 ❌ MAP P122, A1

Located beside a pond studded with ducks, backed by bush and overlooking the Waitangi Treaty Grounds (p120), the Whare Waka (Boathouse) is a top spot for good cafe fare during the day, and to return to for a *hāngi* (earth-oven-cooked) dinner and concert on Tuesday, Thursday, Friday and Sunday evenings from November to March. (☎09-402 7437; www.waitangi.org.nz; Waitangi Treaty Grounds, 1 Tau Henare Dr; mains $15-19.50; ⏱8am-4pm, shorter hours winter; P 👫)

El Cafe   LATIN AMERICAN $
14 ✖ MAP P122, D5

This excellent Chilean-owned cafe has the best coffee in town and terrific breakfast burritos, tacos and baked-egg dishes, such as spicy *huevos rancheros*. The Cuban pulled-pork sandwich is truly a wonderful thing. The fruit smoothies are also great on a warm Bay of Islands day. (☎09-402 7637; www.facebook.com/elcafepaihia; 2 Kings Rd; mains $11-14.50; ⏱8am-4pm Wed-Mon; 📶)

Zane Grey's   SEAFOOD $$
15 ✖ MAP P122, C1

Named after a local fishing legend, and with possibly the biggest deck in all of Northland, Zane Grey's has you covered all day, from traditional breakfasts through to a seafood-focused dinner menu with Asian and Pacific influences. Half of the venue transforms into an enviable bar in the evening with comfy modern lounges ready for conversations fuelled by cocktails or cold beer. (☎09-402 6220; https://zanegreys.co.nz; 69 Marsden Rd; mains $15-38; ⏱8am-10pm)

Hundertwasser in Kawakawa

Eco-architect Friedensreich Hundertwasser put Kawakawa (an otherwise low-key regional town) on the tourism map with his design for the **Kawakawa Public Toilets** (60 Gillies St). These are the most photographed toilets in NZ and are typical Hundertwasser – lots of organic, wavy lines decorated with ceramic mosaics and brightly coloured bottles, and with grass and plants on the roof.

In 2020 a new Memorial Park – the Austrian-born artist lived near Kawakawa in an isolated house without electricity from 1973 until his death in 2000 – was nearly complete (www.hundertwasserpark.com).

Kawakawa also pleases train enthusiasts and kids: there's a steam train to ride on that runs right down the main street. There is also a pair of important Māori sites nearby, a glowworm cave to tour and a buzzing gallery in a converted art-deco theatre.

To get here, drive or take the InterCity coach. It's also an 11km bike ride from Opua on the Pou Herenga Tai Twin Coast Cycle Trail. You can hire bikes by the half-day (near the ferry terminal).

Kayaking, Paihia

Glasshouse Kitchen & Bar
CONTEMPORARY $$$

16 MAP P122, B3

A concise seasonal menu of main dishes showcasing regional produce and local seafood underpinned by subtle Asian influences and one of Northland's best wine lists. (09-402 0111; www.paihiabeach.co.nz; Paihia Beach Resort, 130 Marsden Rd; mains $30-40; 8-10am & 6pm-late)

Shopping

Flying Fish
DESIGN

17 MAP P122, C2

Stylish gifts from New Zealand, from jewellery to merino products and homewares, all quirky, all uniquely Kiwi. (09-402 7755; www.flyingfishdesign.co.nz; Williams Rd)

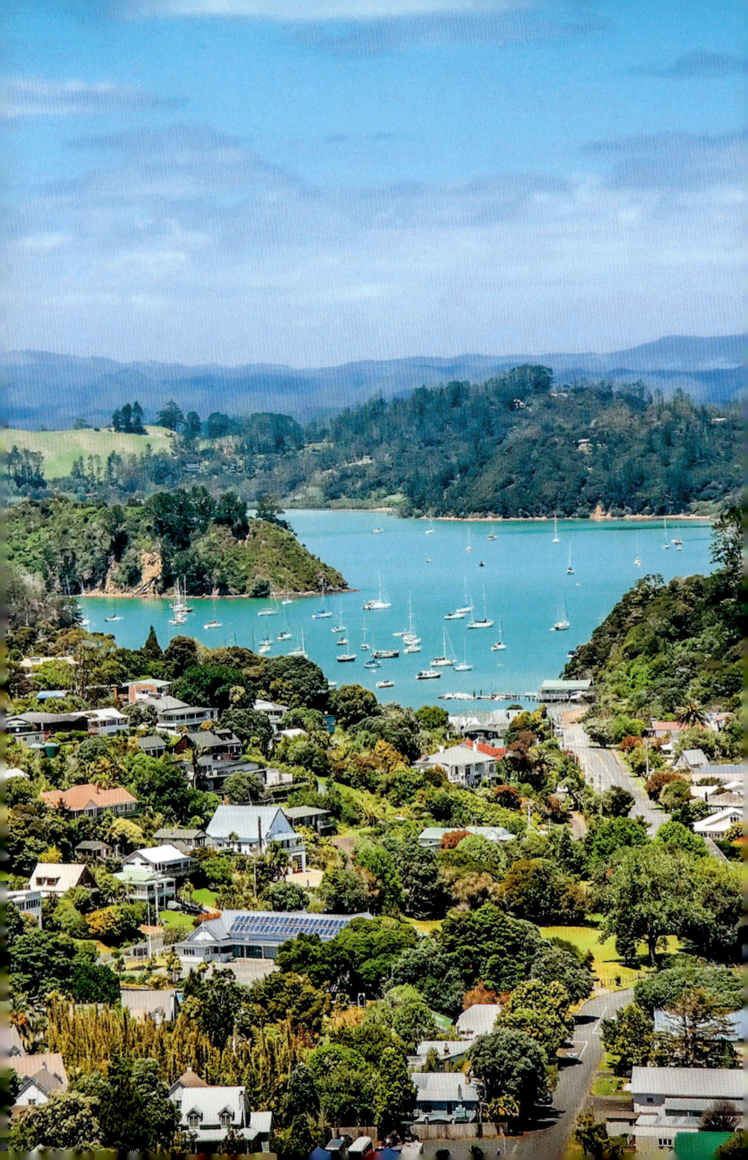

Explore
Russell

Proudly remembered as 'the hellhole of the Pacific', there's little in the way of depravity and debauchery here now. Instead you'll find a historic town made of weatherboard-style colonial buildings dotted with boutiques, souvenir stores and places to eat. The treed hills beyond the harbour's million-dollar houses and holiday accommodation make it hard not to envy the friendly locals who call this slice of paradise home.

The Short List

- **Long Beach (p131)** Sunning yourself on this perfect swimming beach.
- **Pompallier Mission (p131)** Getting a taste of Russell's past with an immersive tour.
- **Omata Estate (p131)** Wine tasting and strolling through the vineyard.
- **Duke of Marlborough Hotel (p133)** Sipping a sundowner at this historic hotel.
- **Hōne's Garden (p133)** Dining alfresco with wood-fired pizza and cold craft beer

Getting There & Around

From Paihia (adult/child return $12/6) from 7am to 9pm. Buy tickets at Paihia's i-SITE. The car ferry (car/motorcycle/passenger $13.50/5.90/1) runs every 10 minutes from Opua (5km from Paihia) between 6am and 9.50pm.

Coming from Auckland you can turn off at Whakapara and follow the Old Russell Road via Helena Bay to reach Russell, or take the ferry.

Russell Map on p130

View from Flagstaff Hill (p131) COLETTE MOORE/SHUTTERSTOCK ©

Russell

130

Map Legend

For reviews see
- ⊙ Sights — p131
- ✕ Eating — p133
- 🔒 Shopping — p135

Map Labels

Streets & Areas:
- Wellington St
- Flagstaff Rd
- Queens (St)
- Prospect St
- James St
- Long Beach Rd
- The Strand
- York St
- Church St
- Beresford St
- Chapel St
- Cass St
- Baker St
- Ashby St
- Oneroa Rd
- Gould St
- Hazard St
- Robertson St
- York St
- Pitt St
- Matauwhi Rd
- Brind Rd
- Ferry to Paihia
- Kororareka Bay

Sights:
- 4 — Flagstaff Hill (Maiki)
- 1
- 3 — Pompallier Mission
- 7 — Russell Museum
- 6 — Christ Church
- 5
- 2
- 8

Eating:
- 11
- 15, 17
- 12
- 16
- 9
- 14
- 10
- 13

Shopping:
- 18
- 19
- 20

Scale: 100 m / 0.05 miles

Sights

Long Beach
BEACH

1 ◎ MAP P130, D4

About 1.5km behind Russell (an easy walk or cycle) is this placid, child-friendly beach. Turn left (facing the sea) to visit **Donkey Bay**, a small cove and unofficial nudist beach. (Oneroa; Long Beach Rd)

Oke Bay
BEACH

2 ◎ MAP P130, C6

It's a bit of a drive (30km) and a short steep walk down to the beach, but worth the effort. There's not a lot of beach when the tide is high so time your visit accordingly.

Pompallier Mission
HISTORIC BUILDING

3 ◎ MAP P130, B6

Built in 1842 to house the Catholic mission's printing press, this rammed-earth building is the mission's last remaining building in the western Pacific, and NZ's oldest industrial building. Over seven years of operation, a staggering 40,000 books were printed here in Māori. Admission includes extremely interesting hands-on tours that lead you through the entire bookmaking process, from tanning animal hides for the covers to setting the type and stitching together the final books. You can visit the gardens only ($7) if you miss out on the tour. (☏ 09-403 9015; www.pompallier.co.nz; 5 The Strand; adult/child $15/free; ⏱ 10am-4pm by guided tour)

Flagstaff Hill
HILL

4 ◎ MAP P130, A1

Overlooking Russell, this is the hill where Hōne Heke chopped down the British flagpole four times. You can drive up, but the epic view over Russell and the harbour rewards a good 1.6km climb. Take the track west from the boat ramp along the beach at low tide, or head up Wellington St. (Maiki; Flagstaff Rd)

Omata Estate
WINERY

5 ◎ MAP P130, C6

With a growing reputation for red wines – especially its old-growth syrah – Omata Estate is one of Northland's finest wineries. To complement the tastings and sea views, pizzas and shared platters are available. The winery is on the road from Russell to the car ferry at Okiato. (☏ 09-403 8007; www.omata.co.nz; 212 Aucks Rd; ⏱ 11am-6pm Oct-May, by appointment Jun-Sep)

Christ Church
CHURCH

6 ◎ MAP P130, C5

English naturalist Charles Darwin made a donation towards the cost of building this, the country's oldest surviving church (1836). The graveyard's biggest memorial commemorates Tamati Waka Nene, a powerful Ngāpuhi chief from the Hokianga who sided against Hōne Heke in the Northland War. The church's wooden exterior has musket and cannonball holes dating from the 1845 battle. (www.oldchurch.org.nz; Church St; admission by donation)

Russell's Infamous Beginnings

Before it was known as a 'hellhole', or even as Russell, this was Kororāreka (Sweet Penguin), a fortified Ngāpuhi village. In the early 19th century the Māori *iwi* here permitted it to become Aotearoa's first European settlement. It quickly became a magnet for rough elements, such as fleeing convicts, whalers and drunken sailors.

By the 1830s dozens of whaling ships at a time were anchored in the harbour. In 1839 Charles Darwin described it as full of 'the very refuse of society' in *The Voyage of the Beagle* (originally known as *Narrative of the Surveying Voyages of His Majesty's Ships* Adventure *and* Beagle).

In 1830 the settlement was the scene of the so-called Girls' War, when two pairs of Māori women were vying for the attention of a whaling captain called Brind. A chance meeting between the rivals on the beach led to verbal abuse and fighting. This minor conflict quickly escalated as family members rallied around to avenge the insult and harm done to their respective relatives. Hundreds were killed and injured over a two-week period before missionaries managed to broker a peace agreement.

After the signing of the Treaty of Waitangi in 1840, Okiato (where the car ferry now leaves from) was the residence of the governor and the temporary capital.

Russell Museum MUSEUM

7 MAP P130, B5

This small museum has a well-presented Māori section, a large 1:5 scale model of Captain Cook's *Endeavour,* a 10-minute video on the town's history and an interactive digital map of Īpipiri, the Māori name for the region. (☏09-403 7701; www.russellmuseum.org.nz; 2 York St; adult/child $10/free; ⏰10am-4pm)

Russell Nature Walks ECOTOUR

8 MAP P130, C6

Located in privately owned native forest 2.5km south of Russell, guided day and night tours provide the opportunity to see native birds, including the weka and tui, and insects such as the weta. Glowworms softly illuminate night tours, and after dark there's the opportunity to hear (and very occasionally see) kiwi. The tours help fund conservation projects. (☏027 908 2334; www.russellnaturewalks.co.nz; 6080 Russell Whakapara Rd; adult/child from $75/40)

Flying Kiwi Parasail PARASAILING

Departs from both Paihia and Russell wharves for NZ's highest parasail (1200ft/366m). (☏09-402 6068; www.parasailnz.com; solo $129, tandem per adult/child $99/69)

Gungha II BOATING

A 20m ocean yacht with a friendly crew, departing from both Russell and Paihia; lunch included. (📞0800 478 900; www.bayofislandssailing.co.nz; day sail $130)

Eating

Hōne's Garden PIZZA $$

9 MAP P130, B5

Head out to Hōne's shaded lantern-lit courtyard for wood-fired pizza (gluten-free available), cold craft beer on tap and a thoroughly easy-going vibe. An expanded menu features tasty wraps and healthy salads. Antipasto platters are good for groups and indecisive diners. (📞022 466 3710; www.facebook.com/honesgarden; 10 York St; pizza $18-25; ⏰noon-10pm Wed-Mon Nov-Apr; 👶)

The Gables CONTEMPORARY $$$

10 MAP P130, B5

Serving Kiwi classics (lamb, beef, seafood), the Gables occupies an 1847 building (formerly a colonial brothel) on the waterfront built using whale vertebrae for foundations. Book a table by the windows for maritime views, and look forward to excellent service and top-notch local produce, including local cheeses. (📞09-403 7670; www.thegablesrestaurant.co.nz; 19 The Strand; mains lunch $22-28, dinner $27-35; ⏰noon-3pm & 5.30-10pm Wed-Mon)

Duke of Marlborough Hotel PUB FOOD $$

11 MAP P130, B4

There's no better spot in Russell to while away a few hours, glass in

Omata Estate (p131)

hand, than the Duke's sunny deck. Thankfully the upmarket bistro food matches the views, plus there's an excellent wine list and a great selection of NZ craft beers. (09-403 7829; www.theduke.co.nz; 35 The Strand; mains lunch $20-39, dinner $26-42; 11.30am-9pm)

Bayside Restaurant & Bar ITALIAN $

13 MAP P130, B4

This waterfront bistro is mostly popular for its location right on the water's edge. The menu ranges from breakfast to burgers, plus wines and craft beers, and children are catered for. A good spot on a sunny day, but skip if it's super busy with day trippers as service is reportedly hit and miss. (www.bayside.nz; 29 The Strand; mains $9-20; 8.30am-9pm)

Sage @ Paroa Bay BISTRO $$

13 MAP P130, C6

With hilltop views over the turquoise waters of the Bay of Islands, this winery restaurant overlooking manicured lawns is worth the drive. A limited mains menu has all the bases covered with quality ingredients and surprising flavours. A side salad comes with *dukkah* spice mix, pickled vegetables and balsamic beetroot, for example. The cheese tasting board is a great afternoon grazing option. (www.paroabay.com/sage; 31 Otamarua Rd; noon-5pm Wed & Thu, to 8pm Fri-Sun)

Greens THAI $$

14 MAP P130, B5

Thai and Indian cuisine feature at this tucked-away diner set back from the street in an old wooden house. With two separate menus

---

Day Trip to Urupukapuka Island

The largest of the bay's islands, Urupukapuka is a tranquil place criss-crossed with walks and surrounded by aquamarine waters. Safe secluded beaches to swim or kayak make this a great option if you want to enjoy the islands without spending too much time on a boat.

Native birds are plentiful thanks to a conservation initiative that has rendered this and all of the neighbouring islands predator-free. A small licensed cafe by the pier serves food and drinks – just don't miss the last ferry back!

Explore NZ (p123) runs several ferries a day to Otehei Bay (adult/child $50/30 return) from Paihia and Russell, though they are less regular in winter.

Bay of Islands Kayaking (021 272 3353; www.bayofislandskayaking.co.nz; tours $90-160) can also arrange kayaking trips to the island with camping gear if you're up for a real adventure.

(and apparently with chefs from Thailand *and* India) meals are rated highly by locals and vegetarian options are strong. It also does takeaway. The sister diner is in Paihia. (☏09-403 7561; www.greensnz.com; 15a York St; mains $19-24; ⏰9am-11pm Mon-Sat)

Newport Chocolates   CAFE $

15 ✖ MAP P130, B4

The sumptuous artisan chocolates are all handmade on site, with flavours such as raspberry, lime and chilli, and, our favourite, caramel and sea salt. It's also a good choice for a decadent hot chocolate or a refreshing frappé. (☏09-403 8402; www.newportchocolates.co.nz; 1 Cass St; chocolates around $3; ⏰10am-6pm Tue-Thu, to 7.30pm Fri & Sat)

Tuk Tuk Bangkok   THAI $$

16 ✖ MAP P130, B4

Thai fabrics adorn the tables and Thai favourites fill the menu of this casual, bar-like place. You won't miss it: a tuk-tuk on the front deck gives the game away. (☏09-403 7111; 19 York St; mains $17-26; ⏰10.30am-11pm; ✈)

Delish   ICE CREAM $

17 ✖ MAP P130, B4

In summer it does a steady trade in ice-cream cones, smoothies and milkshakes. In the depths of winter, this humble coffee counter is the prime local gathering point and the best bet for your morning cuppa and muffin. (☏09-403 8829; 4 Cass St; snacks $3-6; ⏰7.30am-4pm)

Shopping

Wood2Water   HOMEWARES

18 🔒 MAP P130, B5

This eclectic arts and craft store stocks souvenirs and gifts from tea towels to jewellery, framed prints and handcrafted wooden products. Most are local designs, each with a good story to tell. Foodie items include honey, olives and preserves, but also organic ready meals if you're self-catering. (https://felt.co.nz/shop/wood2water; 22 York St; ⏰10am-4pm Wed-Mon)

Caravan Clothing & Home   CLOTHING

19 🔒 MAP P130, B5

A Russell outpost of this Kerikeri-based store selling clothing and homewares in the latest textures, fabrics and colours. Fashionistas will recognise brands like Leon & Harper and Elk, but local makers are also in stock. Expect to leave with a whole new beach-ready outfit. (https://caravanclothinghome.co; Shop 2, 88 Kerikeri Road; ⏰9.30am-5pm Mon-Fri, to 2.30pm Sat)

South Sea Art   ART

20 🔒 MAP P130, B5

Bright acrylic paintings and classic watercolours are the perfect souvenir to remember your Bay of Islands visit. The eclectic collection by local artists at this gallery store can easily be shipped home. (www.southseaart.com; 15 York St; ⏰10am-5.30pm, summer only)

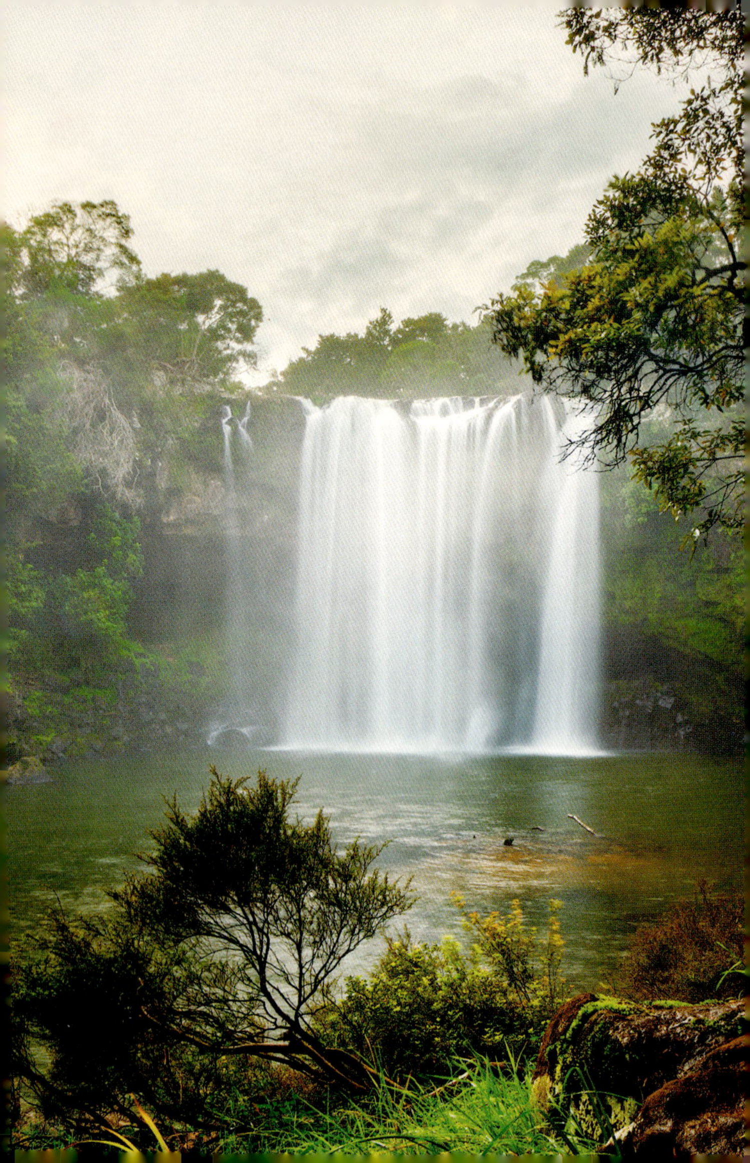

Explore
Kerikeri

Kerikeri is a prosperous inland township surrounded by orchards and vineyards. A snapshot of early Māori and British interaction is offered by a cluster of historic sites centred on the picturesque river basin. In 1819 the powerful Ngāpuhi chief Hongi Hika allowed Reverend Samuel Marsden to start a mission (p139) under the shadow of his Kororipo Pā (p139) here and there's an ongoing campaign to have the area recognised as a Unesco World Heritage Site.

The Short List

- **Kerikeri Mission Station (p139)** *Bringing the early days of settlement to life at the excellent museum.*

- **Kororipo Pā (p139)** *Feeling the mana at this historic Māori site.*

- **Plough & Feather (p141)** *Dining on bistro faves while watching the day slip by.*

- **Kerikeri River Track (p139)** *Walking the 4.6km trail by a river towards its source.*

- **Old Packhouse Market (p141)** *Soaking up the foodie atmosphere at this ramshackle market.*

Getting There & Around

✈ Bay of Islands (Kerikeri) Airport is 8km southwest of town. Air New Zealand flies from Auckland to Kerikeri, your gateway to the Bay of Islands.

🚌 InterCity buses leave opposite the library for Paihia (from $19, 25 minutes) and on to Auckland (from $39, 4¾ hours)

Kerikeri Map on p138

Rainbow Falls (p139) ANUPAM HATUI/SHUTTERSTOCK ©

Kerikeri

For reviews see
- Sights p139
- Eating p141
- Drinking p143
- Entertainment p143
- Shopping p143

Sights

Kerikeri Mission Station
HISTORIC SITE

1 ◎ MAP P138, E4

Two of the nation's most significant buildings nestle side by side on the banks of Kerikeri Basin. Start at the **Stone Store**, NZ's oldest stone building (1836). Upstairs there's an interesting little museum, while downstairs the shop sells Kiwiana gifts as well as the type of wood and leather goods that used to be stocked here in the 19th century. Tours of neighbouring **Kemp House** depart from here. Built by the missionaries in 1822, this humble yet pretty wooden Georgian-style house is NZ's oldest building.

The house is encircled by heritage gardens, and the mature fruit trees scattered all around the river basin are the remnants of the mission's original orchard. In summer, the Honey House Cafe operates from a neighbouring cottage. (☏09-407 9236; www.historic.org.nz; 246 Kerikeri Rd; museum $8, house tour $12, combined $15, children free; ⏰10am-5pm Nov-Apr, to 4pm May-Oct; 👫)

Kororipo Pā
HISTORIC SITE

2 ◎ MAP P138, F4

Just up the hill from Kerikeri Mission Station is a marked historical walk that leads to the site of Hongi Hika's *pā* (fortress) and village. Little remains aside from the terracing that once supported wooden palisades. Huge war parties once departed from here, terrorising much of the North Island and slaughtering thousands during the Musket Wars. The role of missionaries in arming Ngāpuhi remains controversial. The walk emerges near the cute wooden St James Anglican Church (1878). (Kerikeri Rd; admission free; 👫)

Kerikeri River Track
WALKING

3 ◎ MAP P138, E4

Starting from Kerikeri Basin, this 4.6km track leads through beautiful native bush past Wharepuke Falls and the **Fairy Pools** to the Rainbow Falls, where even on dim days the 27m drop conjures dancing rainbows. Alternatively, you can reach Rainbow Falls from Rainbow Falls Rd.

Rainbow Falls
WATERFALL

4 ◎ MAP P138, D1

An impressive waterfall on the river that can also be accessed via the road. A historic tea house is close by for those walking from the river basin and needing a refreshment.

Wharepuke Falls
WATERFALL

5 ◎ MAP P138, E2

What it lacks in height this attractive waterfall makes up for in breadth. It's accessed from the Kerikeri River Track.

Rewa's Village
MUSEUM

6 ◎ MAP P138, F4

If you had a hard time imagining nearby Kororipo Pā in its original state, take the footbridge across

Artisans of Kerikeri

You'd be forgiven for thinking that everyone in Kerikeri is involved in some small-scale artisanal enterprise, given the bombardment of craft shops on the way into town. A little further afield, a handful of vineyards are doing their best to stake Northland's claim as a wine region. The little-known red grape chambourcin has proved particularly suited to the region's subtropical humidity, along with pinotage and syrah.

Look out for the *Art & Craft Trail* and *Wine Trail* brochures. Here are our tasty recommendations:

Ake Ake Wine tastings are $8, free with a purchase of wine.

Cottle Hill Wine, port and grappa tastings, free with a purchase.

Get Fudged & Keriblue Ceramics (p143) An unusual pairing of ceramics and big, decadent slabs of fudge.

Makana Confections (p143) Artisan chocolate factory with a cafe attached.

Marsden Estate (p142) Wine tastings and lunch on the terrace.

---

the river to this mock-up of a traditional Māori fishing village. Opening hours can be hit and miss, and it's in need of some maintenance. (☎09-407 6454; www.rewasvillage.co.nz; 1 Landing Rd; adult/child $10/5; ◷10am-4pm)

Charlie's Rock SWIMMING HOLE
7 ◉ MAP P138, F3

This secret swimming hole is not easy to find, but those who do are rewarded with a plunge in the crisp, cold water. Ask the locals how to get here; you follow Waipara Stream from the Croquet Club opposite the car park on Landing Rd.

Northland Paddleboarding WATER SPORTS

Lessons and guided stand-up paddles departing from various locations around Kerikeri. A great way to get out on the water here, where most of the town is land based. (☎027 777 1035; www.northlandpaddleboarding.co.nz; beginner lessons per hour $60)

Cottle Hill WINERY
8 ◉ MAP P138, B3

Call into the cellar door for a tasting of wine, port and grappa. It's just off SH10 south of Kerikeri. (☎09-407 5203; www.cottlehill.co.nz; 28 Cottle Hill Dr; tastings $5, free with purchase; ◷10am-5pm Wed-Sun)

Eating

Ake Ake BRITISH, FRENCH $$
9   MAP P138, A1

At this upmarket winery restaurant, the rural setting is complemented by hearty but sophisticated country fare, such as lamb shanks, wild game pie, confit duck and steak. The Sunday roasts are legendary. After lunch, work off some of the calories on the 1km self-guided trail through the vineyard. (09-407 8230; www.akeakevineyard.co.nz; 165 Waimate North Rd; mains $30-36; 11.45am-2pm & 5.45-8pm Mon-Sat, lunch only Sun, tastings 10am-4.30pm;)

Plough & Feather BISTRO $$
10   MAP P138, E4

Kerikeri's best located and most upmarket restaurant occupies an old homestead right on the basin (book ahead for a table on the veranda). Mains run the gamut of bistro favourites like burgers, steak and fish of the day, plus a good selection of vegan options. There's also an excellent range of New Zealand craft beers. (09-407 8479; www.ploughandfeather.co.nz; 215 Kerikeri Rd; mains lunch $12-24, dinner $30-32; 9am-10pm summer)

Rusty Tractor CAFE $$
11   MAP P138, B2

As decadent breakfasts go, Rusty Tractor's doughnuts with crème fraiche and berries take some beating. There are healthier options, too, and the coffee's up with the best in Kerikeri. Otherwise, treat yourself to a glass of wine while the kids play on the rocket-ship slide on the back lawn. (09-407 3322; www.rustytractorcafe.co.nz; 582 Kerikeri Rd; mains breakfast $17-20, lunch $20-26; 8am-3pm;)

Old Packhouse Market MARKET $
12   MAP P138, B2

Local artisans, winemakers and farmers sell their goodies at this market in an old fruit-packing shed on the outskirts of town. It's the spot for a grazing breakfast on Saturdays, and check its calendar for themed Thursday-night markets. (09-401 9588; www.facebook.com/theoldpackhousemarket; 505 Kerikeri Rd; 8am-1.30pm Sat)

Kerikeri Mission Station (p139)

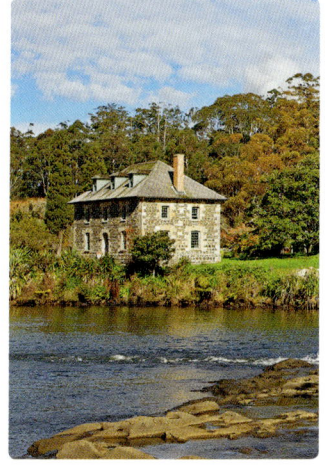

DAVID STEELEY/SHUTTERSTOCK ©

Māha
THAI, EUROPEAN $$$

13 MAP P138, E3

With one foot in Europe, the other in Japan and its head in the lush vegetation of Wharepuke Subtropical Gardens, this is Kerikeri's most unusual and inspired eatery. Adjacent is the interesting Wharepuke Print Studio. (09-945 6551; www.maharestaurant.co.nz; 190 Kerikeri Rd; mains $20-40; 11am-late Tue-Sat)

Marsden Estate
CONTEMPORARY $$

14 MAP P138, A2

The interior of this winery restaurant is large and featureless so opt for the covered terrace at the rear, which has wonderful views over the vines and a pretty pond. Cooked breakfasts give way to sophisticated lunches that match prime local produce with flavours from all over the world. (09-407 9398; www.marsdenestate.co.nz; 56 Wiroa Rd; mains breakfast $18-23, lunch $28-38; cellar door 10am-5pm;)

Cafe Jerusalem
ISRAELI $$

15 MAP P138, C3

Northland's best falafels, lamb shawarma and meze platters, all served with a smile and a social vibe. Most mains come with rice, pitta bread, tabouli and a salad. Try the shakshuka (baked eggs in a spicy tomato sauce) for a hearty brunch. (09-407 1001; www.cafejerusalem.co.nz; Village Mall, 85 Kerikeri Rd; mains $18.50-22.50; 10am-late Mon-Sat)

Kiwi Spotting at Aroha Island

Just north of town is a small 12-hectare self-managed wildlife reserve and ecological centre, **Aroha Island** (*aroha* meaning 'love'; www.arohaisland.co.nz), where conservation and wildlife protection is the focus.

There's a small informative visitor centre to learn more about North Island brown kiwis, their habits and their story of survival after predators were introduced to mainland New Zealand.

Self-guided walks around the island afford you the chance to see these shy birds in the wild Those lucky to see or hear a kiwi – as well as other native birdlife – note the time and place in the shared visitors book.

After dark is of course the best time to see these elusive flightless birds, and special kit (red lights only – they won't come out if you're shining a bright torch around) can be hired for a small fee.

It's a well-signposted 10km drive from Kerikeri to the permanent causeway through the mangroves to the island.

Accommodation is also available in newly renovated cottages or in a simple grass camping ground by the sea, if you want to stay and maximise your best chance of seeing real kiwis.

Black Olive PIZZA
16 MAP P138, B3

This unassuming, family-friendly restaurant delivers when it comes to delicious pizzas (gluten-free available) topped with fresh produce and free-range meats. Bistro mains complement the pizza options, from lamb shank to fish and chips. And the outside deck is a great option for families. (09-407 9693; www.theblackolive.net; 308 Kerikeri Rd; 4pm-late Tue-Sun;)

Cafe Zest & the Waffle Room CAFE $$
17 MAP P138, C3

If sugar is your weakness, the Waffle Room may be your undoing. Avoid temptation by grabbing a table in the cafe side of Zest and averting your eyes from the heavily laden waffles wafting past. The outside tables are a great spot to soak up the afternoon sun. (09-407 7164; 73 Kerikeri Rd; mains $13-22; 7.30am-4pm Mon-Fri, to 2pm Sat & Sun)

Drinking

La Taza Del Diablo BAR
18 MAP P138, B3

This Mexican-style bar is about as energetic and raffish as buttoned-down Kerikeri gets, with a decent selection of tequila, Mexican beers and, just maybe, Northland's best margaritas. Tacos, enchiladas and chimichangas all feature on the bar-snacks menu, and occasional live gigs sometimes raise the roof in this genteel town. (09-407 3912; www.facebook.com/eltazadeldiablo; 3 Homestead Rd; 11.30am-late Wed-Sun;)

Entertainment

Cathay Cinemas CINEMA
19 MAP P138, B3

Hollywood new releases and arthouse flicks in an historic 1930s weatherboard building. (09-407 4428; www.cathaycinemas.co.nz; 27 Hobson Ave)

Shopping

Makana Confections CHOCOLATE
20 MAP P138, B2

Sample a chocolate in the shop and watch the artisans at work through the factory window. There's also a cafe attached, selling pastries and gelato. (09-407 6800; www.makana.co.nz; 504 Kerikeri Rd; 9am-5.30pm)

Little Black Gallery ART
21 MAP P138, A2

Off the beaten track along a bamboo-lined lane, this tiny stylish gallery sells unique jewellery, art and gifts. (www.littleblackgallery.co.nz; 394b Kerikeri Rd; 10.30am-4pm Tue-Sat, shorter hours winter)

Get Fudged & Keriblue Ceramics Studio CERAMICS
22 MAP P138, B1

An unusual pairing of ceramics and slabs of fudge in a colourful studio. (09-407 1111; www.kerikblueceramics.co.nz; 1691 SH10; 9am-5pm)

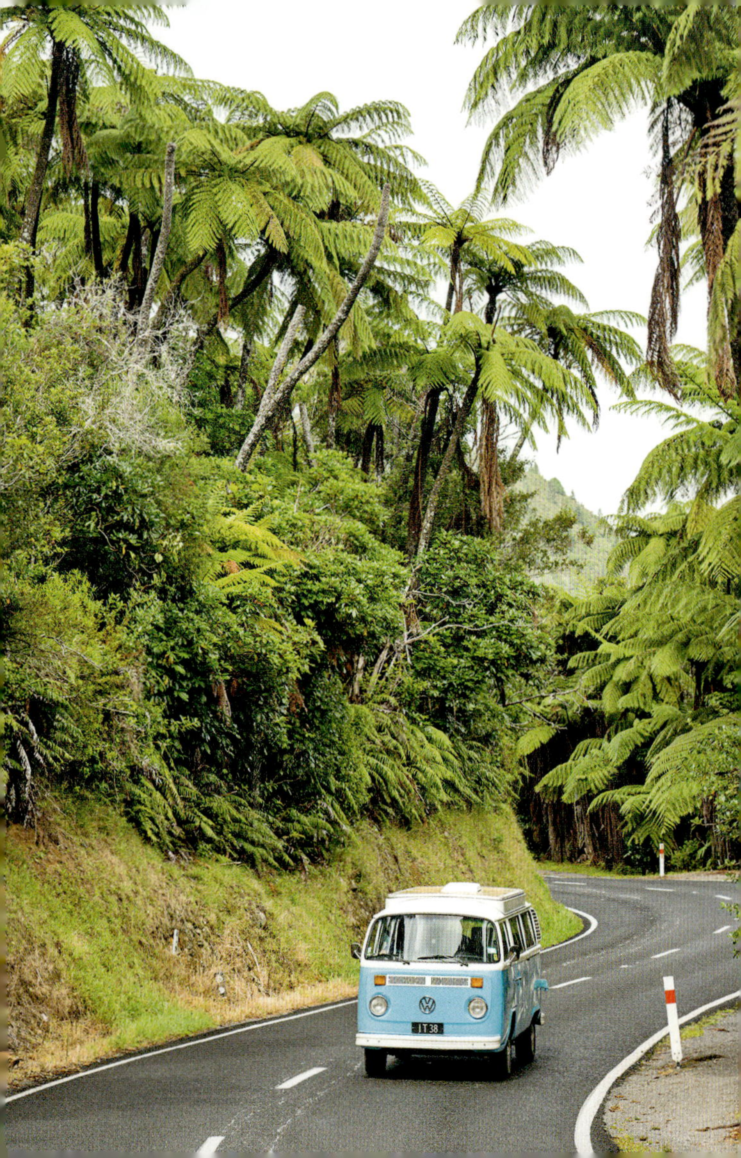
IT38

Survival Guide

Before You Go — 146
Book Your Stay — 146
When to Go — 146

Arriving in Auckland — 147
Auckland Airport (AKL) — 147
Queens Wharf & Princes Wharf Cruise Terminals — 148

Getting Around — 148
Bus — 148
Ferry — 148
Taxi — 149
Ride-Sharing Apps — 149
Train — 149

Essential Information — 149
Accessible Travel — 149
Business Hours — 149
Discount Cards — 149
Electricity — 150
LGBTQI+ Travellers — 150
Mobile Phones — 151
Money — 151
Public Holidays — 152
Safe Travel — 152
Toilets — 152
Tourist Information — 152
Visas — 153

Waitākere Ranges (p115), West Auckland JUSTIN FOULKES/LONELY PLANET ©

Before You Go

Book Your Stay

o Auckland's city centre has a smattering of luxury hotels including international chains.

o For B&B accommodation, Ponsonby, Mt Eden and Parnell are all recommended, and Devonport has heritage B&Bs a relaxing ferry ride from the city.

o The city's best backpacker hostels are largely in inner suburbs such as Mt Eden and Ponsonby.

o Booking two to three months ahead is recommended from December to April.

o Accommodation routinely books out when there is a major concert or sporting events in the city. Check dates carefully.

Useful Websites

Lonely Planet (www.lonelyplanet.com/new-zealand/auckland/hotels) Recommendations and bookings.

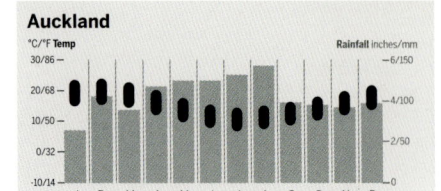

Auckland

When to Go

o **Feb–Apr** The most settled weather of the year. Children have gone back to school and there are many festivals held across these months.

o **May–Oct** A quieter time with Auckland's winter and autumn attractions including museums and galleries, and good restaurants, cafes and bars. Wrap up warmly for boat trips.

o **Dec–Jan** Warm weather, although the climate is often fickle and Auckland's summer months still average eight days of rain. Across Christmas and New Year some cafes and restaurants may close.

Bookabach (www.bookabach.co.nz) Good online resource for rental holiday homes, especially on Waiheke and Great Barrier and in the Bay of Islands.

Best Budget

Fossil Bay Lodge (www.fossilbaylodge.co.nz) Comfortable Waiheke Island cabins and glamping.

Haka Lodge (www.hakalodges.com) Modern hostel right on energetic Karangahape Rd.

Verandahs (www.verandahs.co.nz) Friendly hostel in a heritage Ponsonby villa.

Piha Beachstay – Jandal Palace (www.pihabeachstay.co.nz) Ecofriendly stay in sleepy Piha.

Seabeds (www.seabeds.co.nz) Stylish and welcoming Paihia hostel.

Best Midrange

Parituhu (www.parituhu.co.nz) Welcoming Devonport B&B with well-travelled hosts.

Haka Hotel (https://hakahotels.co.nz) Modern, well-equipped and centrally located.

Abaco on Jervois (www.abaco.co.nz) Excellent motel accommodation conveniently close to public transport.

Ponsonby Manor (www.ponsonbymanor.co.nz) Stylish and good-value B&B.

Wharepuke Subtropical Accommodation (www.accommodation-bay-of-islands.co.nz) Relaxed garden cottages amid Kerikeri palms.

Best Top End

Hotel DeBrett (www.hoteldebrett.com) Hip heritage bolthole in central Auckland.

Ascot Parnell (www.ascotparnell.com) Luxury apartment living in Parnell.

Sofitel Auckland Viaduct Harbour (www.sofitel-auckland.com) International class right on the harbour.

Franklin 38 (www.franklin38.co.nz) Ultra-luxe suites in a heritage Ponsonby villa.

Arcadia Lodge (www.arcadialodge.co.nz) Luxury and brilliant views in Russell.

Arriving in Auckland

Auckland Airport (AKL)

Auckland's **airport** (AKL; 09-275 0789; www.aucklandairport.co.nz; Ray Emery Dr, Māngere) is 21km south of the city centre. It has separate international and domestic terminals a 10-minute walk from each other via a signposted footpath. A free shuttle service between the terminals operates every 15 minutes between 5am and 10.30pm. Both terminals have left-luggage facilities, free wi-fi access, bars and eateries, ATMs and car-rental desks.

Bus

Skybus (09-222 0084; www.skybus.co.nz; one way/return adult $17/32, child $2/4;) Runs bright-red buses between the airport terminals and the city, every 10 to 15 minutes from 5.15am to 7pm and around half-hourly throughout the night. Stops include Mt Eden Rd or Dominion Rd, Symonds St, Queen St and Britomart. Reservations are not required; buy a ticket from the driver, the airport kiosk or online. There is a small discount for pre-booking online. Buses leave from outside door 8 at the international terminal

Taxi & Ride Share

The fastest way to travel from the airport to the city centre, taxis take around 25 to 50 minutes and cost from $50 to $80 depending on traffic. Only licensed companies can operate from the designated ranks outside door 8 in the Arrivals area. Ride-share operators including Uber, Ola

Dos & Don'ts

- Say 'Thank you' to your bus driver when getting off a bus. It'll definitely be appreciated.

- Greetings are informal in social settings and first names are commonly used in initial introductions.

- The use of te reo Māori (Māori language) is becoming more mainstream in NZ media. A good place for visitors to start is 'Kia ora' ('Hello').

- Purchase local products. New Zealanders are very proud of their country's independence and individuality.

and Zoomy all operate from outside door 11 of the Arrivals area.

Shuttle

Super Shuttle (09-522 5100; www.supershuttle.co.nz) A convenient door-to-door shuttle service between the airport and city hotels. Charges are from $17.50 to $25 per person depending on group size. Book online prior to arrival or direct with the driver.

Queens Wharf & Princes Wharf Cruise Terminals

Auckland is growing in popularity as a cruising port, and all visiting ships dock at either Queens Wharf or Princes Wharf, two adjacent facilities in the heart of downtown Auckland at the waterfront end of Queen St.

Getting Around

Bus

- The most useful services are the environmentally friendly Link Buses that loop in both directions around three routes (taking in many of the major sights) from 7am to 11pm:

City Link (adult/child $1/50c, every seven to 10 minutes) Wynyard, Britomart, Queen St, Karangahape Rd.

Inner Link (adult/child $3.50/2, every 10 to 15 minutes) Queen St, SkyCity, Victoria Park, Ponsonby Rd, Karangahape Rd, Museum, Newmarket, Parnell and Britomart.

Outer Link (maximum $5.50, every 15 minutes) Art Gallery, Ponsonby, Herne Bay, Westmere, MOTAT 2, Pt Chevalier, Mt Albert, St Lukes Mall, Mt Eden, Newmarket, Museum, Parnell, University.

Ferry

Fullers (09-367 9111; www.fullers.co.nz; return adult/child $42/21; 5.20am-11.45pm Mon-Fri, 6.15am-11.45pm Sat, 7am-10.30pm Sun) Runs frequent passenger ferries from Auckland's Ferry Building to Matiatia Wharf (40 minutes) on Waiheke Island, some via Devonport (adding an extra 10 minutes to the journey time).

Sealink (0800 732 546; www.sealink.co.nz; return adult/child/motorcycle $39/20/175/72; 6am-6pm) Runs car ferries to Kennedy Point on Waiheke Island, mainly from Half Moon

Bay in east Auckland (45 to 60 minutes, at least hourly), but some leave from Wynyard Wharf in the city (60 to 80 minutes, three per day). Sealink also operates car ferries to Great Barrier Island, but it's both cheaper and faster to fly (30 minutes from Auckland Airport).

Taxi

○ Auckland's many taxis usually operate from ranks and outside hotels, but they also cruise popular areas. **Auckland Co-op Taxis** (09-300 3000; www.cooptaxi.co.nz) is one of the biggest companies. Cab companies set their own fares, so there's some variance in rates. There's a surcharge for transport to and from the airport and cruise ships, and for phone bookings.

Ride-Sharing Apps

Uber and local competitors Ola and Zoomy are available in Auckland but not in the Bay of Islands. Expect significant surge pricing during rush hour and after concerts and major sporting events. Taxis are usually the cheaper option during these times.

Train

Auckland's limited train network has just four routes, and for short-term visitors to the city the western line from Britomart to Swanson, stopping at both Kingsland and Morningside, is of most convenience. Buy a ticket (adult/child $5.50/3) from the machines or ticket offices at the Britomart Transport Centre. Note that construction of Auckland's massive City Rail Link project is scheduled to continue until late 2024. Be prepared for some disruption to street access and traffic in various parts of the central city as work continues.

Essential Information

Accessible Travel

Auckland accommodation generally caters fairly well for travellers with disabilities, with many places equipped with wheelchair-accessible rooms. Many tourist attractions similarly provide wheelchair access and wheelchair-friendly taxis can be ordered. Pedestrian crossings cater to both hearing- and sight-impaired people with visual and aural signals. Download Lonely Planet's free Accessible Travel guides from https://shop.lonelyplanet.com/categories/accessible-travel.

Business Hours

Banks 9.30am–4.30pm Monday to Friday

Cafes 8am–4pm

Pubs and bars noon–late

Restaurants noon–2.30pm and 6pm–10pm

Shops 9am–6pm Monday to Saturday, 11am–4pm Sunday

Discount Cards

○ The internationally recognised **International Student Identity Card** is produced by the ISIC Association (www.isic.org), and issued to full-time students aged 12 and over. It provides discounts on accommodation, transport and admission to attractions. The same folks also produce the **International Youth Travel Card**, available to travellers aged under 31 who are not full-time students, with equivalent benefits to the ISIC. Also similar is the **International Teacher Identity Card**, available to teaching professionals. All three cards ($30 each) are available online as virtual cards at www.isiccard.co.nz.

○ The **New Zealand Card** (www.newzealandcard.com) is a $35 discount pass that'll score you between 5% and 50% off a range of accommodation, tours, sights and activities. Browse participating businesses before you buy. It offers a range of discounts, especially in the Bay of Islands.

○ Travellers aged over 60 with some form of identification (eg an official seniors card from your home country) are often eligible for concession prices.

Electricity

Type I
230V/50Hz

LGBTQI+ Travellers

The Queen City (as it's known for completely coincidental reasons) has by far NZ's biggest gay population, with the bright lights attracting gay and lesbian Kiwis from all over the country. However, the even brighter lights of Sydney eventually steal many of the 30- to 40-somethings, leaving a gap in the demographic. There are very few gay venues, and they only really kick off on the weekends. For the latest, see the monthly magazine *Express* (available from gay venues) or visit the website www.gayexpress.co.nz.

The big event on the calendar is February's **Auckland Pride Festival** (www.aucklandpride.org.nz; ⏲Feb). It's also well worth watching out for are the regular parties held by Urge Events (www.facebook.com/urgebar); the only reliably fun and sexy nights out for the over-30s, they book out quickly.

Venues change with alarming regularity, but these ones were the stayers at the time of writing:

Family (Map p86, G5; ☏09-309 0213; 270 Karangahape Rd; ⏲9am-4am) Trashy, brash and extremely young, Family gets crammed on weekends, with drag hosts and dancing into the wee hours, both at the back of the ground-level bar and in the club downstairs.

Staircase (Map p86, H5; ☏09-303 1661; www.facebook.com/Staircasebar; 25 Cross St; ⏲4.30-

Money-Saving Tips

○ For longer stays in the city, an AT HOP smartcard ($10, www.athop.co.nz) provides discounts of at least 20% on most buses, trains and ferries.

○ Stay in slightly less-central suburbs like Sandringham, Epsom, Morningside or St Heliers and use public transport to get to and from the central city.

○ Eat at Auckland's night markets (www.aucklandnightmarkets.co.nz), especially the two central locations.

○ www.moviesinparks.co.nz and www.musicinparks.co.nz detail free screenings and concerts from January to April.

11pm Tue-Thu, to 4am Fri & Sat, 5-9pm Sun) Inclusive and welcoming bar with occasional quiz nights and drag shows, and a well-frequented dance floor. Wider age range than other venues. Check out the Facebook page to see what's on.

Eagle (Map p86, G5; ☏ 09-309 4979; www.facebook.com/the.eagle.bar; 259 Karangahape Rd; ⏰ 4pm-1am Mon, Tue & Sun, to 2am Wed & Thu, to 4am Fri & Sat) A cosy place for a quiet drink early in the evening, getting more raucous as the night progresses. Get in quick to put your picks on the video jukebox or prepare for an entire evening of Kylie and Taylor.

Mobile Phones

○ Bring your own unlocked phone and use a prepaid service with a local SIM card (rather than pay for expensive global roaming on your home network).

○ Vodafone (www.vodafone.co.nz), Spark (www.spark.co.nz) and 2Degrees (www.2degrees.co.nz) are New Zealand's three mobile phone networks. Both Spark and Vodafone have shops in the Arrivals area of Auckland Airport. All three have stores in central Auckland and Newmarket.

○ Travel SIM packages for visitors to New Zealand begin at $30 and include calling and messaging to 16 overseas countries.

Money

ATMs

ATMS are widespread in Auckland and the Bay of Islands and are usually located at the same address as banks.

Eftpos

Many New Zealand businesses use Eftpos (electronic funds transfer at point of sale), allowing you to use your bank card (credit or debit) to make direct purchases and it's often possible to withdraw cash as well. Eftpos is available practically everywhere: just like at an ATM, you'll need a PIN.

Credit Cards

○ Credit cards (Visa, MasterCard) are widely accepted for everything from a cold beer to a bungy jump, and are pretty much essential for car hire.

○ Credit cards can also be used for over-the-counter cash advances at banks and from ATMs, but be aware that such transactions incur charges. Diners Club and American Express cards are not as widely accepted.

○ It is becoming increasingly widespread for some businesses to charge an additional surcharge from 1% to 3% to offset the service fee that credit-card companies charge merchants.

Tipping

○ Tipping is completely optional in NZ, but your activity guide or tour group leader will happily accept tips; up to $10 is fine.

○ In restaurants, the total on your bill is all you need to pay (though sometimes a service charge is factored in). Reward extra good service with a tip of around 10%. For cafes, it's becoming common to add change from a transaction to a tip jar.

Public Holidays

New Zealand's main public holidays are as follows:

New Year 1 and 2 January

Waitangi Day 6 February

Easter Good Friday and Easter Monday March/April

Anzac Day 25 April

Queen's Birthday First Monday in June

Labour Day Fourth Monday in October

Christmas Day 25 December

Boxing Day 26 December

In addition to these dates, Auckland celebrates the city's **Anniversary Day** on the fourth Monday in January.

Safe Travel

Auckland isn't a particularly dangerous place, but it pays to keep your wits about you if you're walking alone late at night. Alcohol-fuelled aggression isn't uncommon around the Viaduct and the bottom of the city centre in the early hours on the weekend. Otherwise, the main dangers are all road related, with Aucklanders notorious for running red lights, failing to indicate and failing to allow other drivers to change lanes.

Toilets

Public toilets are located at the Silo Park end of Wynyard Quarter, in the Central City Library in Lorne St, and the Britomart Transport Centre. Shopping malls and pubs are also convenient options.

Tourist Information

Auckland International Airport i-SITE (☏ 09-365 9925; www.aucklandnz.com; International Arrivals Hall; ⊙ 6.30am-10pm)

Cornwall Park Information Centre (☎ 09-630 8485; www.cornwallpark.co.nz; Huia Lodge, Michael Horton Dr; ⓘ 10am-4pm)

Devonport Information Centre (www.devonport.co.nz; The Arcade, 15 Victoria Rd; ⓘ 10am-2pm; 🛜)

Karanga Kiosk (Map p52, C2; ☎ 09-365 1290; cnr Jellicoe & Halsey Sts, Wynyard Quarter; ⓘ 9.30am-4.30pm) This volunteer-run centre dispenses information on goings-on around the waterfront.

Princes Wharf i-SITE (Map p52, F2; ☎ 09-365 9914; www.aucklandnz.com; Princes Wharf; ⓘ 9am-5pm) Auckland's main official information centre, incorporating the **DOC Auckland Visitor Centre** (Map p52, F2; ☎ 09-379 6476; www.doc.govt.nz; Princes Wharf; ⓘ 9am-5pm).

SkyCity i-SITE (Map p34, A5; ☎ 09-365 9918; www.aucklandnz.com; SkyCity Atrium, cnr Victoria & Federal Sts; ⓘ 9am-5pm)

Visas

○ Visitors from 60 countries must apply online for an **NZeTA** (New Zealand Electronic Travel Authority) a minimum of 72 hours before travelling to the country. Once approved the NZeTA is valid for multiple visits of up to three months for a period of two years. Australian passport holders and permanent residents of some South Pacific nations are exempt.

○ Apply online at www.immigration.govt.nz or by using Immigration NZ's mobile app ($9).

○ An additional fee of $35 per person is charged at the same time. This International Visitor Conservation and Tourism Levy (IVL) is used to support NZ's tourism infrastructure and also help to protect the country's natural environment.

Behind the Scenes

Send Us Your Feedback

We love to hear from travellers – your comments help make our books better. We read every word, and we guarantee that your feedback goes straight to the authors. Visit **lonelyplanet.com/contact** to submit your updates and suggestions.

Note: We may edit, reproduce and incorporate your comments in Lonely Planet products such as guidebooks, websites and digital products, so let us know if you don't want your comments reproduced or your name acknowledged. For a copy of our privacy policy visit lonelyplanet.com/privacy.

Brett's Thanks

Cheers to Carol, Marc and Debi, who were enthusiastic research assistants, and Mum and Dad for invaluable support at a busy time. Thanks to my NZ co-authors, Peter, Tasmin, Andrew, Charles and Monique, and to Kat and Angela in Melbourne for answering all my questions.

Tasmin's Thanks

Thanks to my NZ co-writers, especially Brett and Peter for the mentoring on the road and back at my desk. Cheers to Clare Loudon and Dave Tucker for putting up with me in Auckland. Thanks to my gorgeous family Hugh, Willa and Maisie for the love and support this year. Finally, huge thanks to *all* the Lonely Planet folk who made this title: your quest for excellence in publishing inspires me on every trip.

Acknowledgements

Cover photograph: Auckland city centre, Yoshio Tomii/Getty Images ©

This Book

This 1st edition of Lonely Planet's *Pocket Auckland & the Bay of Islands* guidebook was researched and written by Brett Atkinson and Tasmin Waby. This guidebook was produced by the following:

Senior Product Editors Kate Chapman, Kathryn Rowan

Regional Senior Cartographer Diana Von Holdt

Product Editor James Appleton

Book Designer Katherine Marsh

Assisting Cartographer Anthony Phelan

Assisting Editors Gemma Graham, Rosie Nicholson, Kristin Odijk, Mani Ramaswamy, Fionnuala Twomey, Anna Tyler, Simon Williamson

Assisting Book Designer Wibowo Rusli

Cover Researcher Brendan Dempsey-Spencer

Thanks to Ronan Abayawickrema, Angela Tinson

Index

See also separate subindexes for:

- **Eating p157**
- **Drinking p158**
- **Entertainment p159**
- **Shopping p159**

A

accessible travel 149
accommodation 146-7
activities 21, *see also individual activities*
Albert Park 36
All Blacks 67
Aotea Square 36
Aroha Island 142
art galleries 17, 92
ATMs 151
Auckland Adventure Jet 38
Auckland Art Gallery 32-3
Auckland Beer Mile 66
Auckland Bridge Climb & Bungy 37
Auckland Domain 74
Auckland Hop On, Hop Off Explorer 53-4
Auckland Museum 70-1
Auckland on Water Boat Show 54
Auckland Sea Kayaks 109
Auckland Seaplanes 53

Sights 000
Map Pages 000

Auckland Zoo 54
Awesome NZ 125

B

bathrooms 152
Bay of Islands 116-43, **116**
Bay of Islands Kayaking 134
beaches 16
  Great Barrier Island 106
  West Auckland 111-12
beer 12-13, 66
bicycling 125
Big Foody Food Tour 37
Black Caps 67
boat travel 148-9
Britomart 31-47, 45-7, **34-5**
  food 38-42
  shopping 47
  sights 36-8
  transport 31
bus travel 148
Bush & Beach 111
business hours 149

C

cell phones 151
Charlie's Rock 140
children, travel with 18

Christ Church 131
city centre 31-47, **34-5**
  drinking 42-5
  entertainment 45-7
  food 38-42
  shopping 47
  sights 32-3, 36-8
  transport 31
Civic Theatre 36
climate 146
Coast to Coast Walkway 57
Coastal Kayakers 123
Connells Bay 99
Cornwall Park 81
costs 24, 149-50, 151
Cottle Hill 140
craft beer 12-13, 66
Crazy Horse Trike Tours 105
credit cards 152
cricket 67
currency 24
cycling 125

D

dangers, *see* safety
Devonport 44
disabilities, travellers with 149
Diwali Festival of Lights 40
Donkey Bay 131

drinking & nightlife 12-13, *see also individual neighbourhoods*, Drinking subindex

E

EcoZip Adventures 101
Eden Garden 64
electricity 150
entertainment, *see* Entertainment subindex
events 40, 54
Ewelme Cottage 74
Explore 53
Explore NZ 123

F

Fairy Pools 139
Fergs Kayaks 109
Ferry Building 43
ferry travel 148-9
festivals 40, 54
Flagstaff Hill 131
Flying Kiwi Parasail 123, 132
food 10-11, *see also individual neighbourhoods*, Eating subindex
Fullers 360 38
Fullers Great Sights 123-4

G

gay travellers 150-1
Go Great Barrier Island 105
Good Heavens 106
Great Barrier Island 104-7, **107**
Gungha II 133

H

Haruru Falls 124
Hauraki Gulf 43
highlights 6-9
Highwic 74-5
hiking 105-6
history 20
holidays 152
Holy Trinity Cathedral 74
Hooked on Barrier 105

I

itineraries 22-3

K

Kaitoke Hot Springs Track 106
Karangahape Rd 83-95, **86-7**
 drinking 90-3
 entertainment 93-4
 food 88-90, 91
 shopping 94-5
 transport 83
kauri 115
Kawakawa 126
Kelly Tarlton's Sea Life Aquarium 109

Sights 000
Map Pages **000**

Kerikeri 137-43, **138**
 drinking 143
 eating 141-3
 entertainment 143
 shopping 140, 143
 sights 139-40
 transport 137
Kerikeri Mission Station 139
Kerikeri River Track 139
Kinder House 74
Kingsland 59-67, **62-3**
 drinking 66-7
 entertainment 67
 food 64-6
 shopping 67
 transport 59
kiwis 43, 142
Kororipo Pā 139

L

language 24
Lantern Festival 40
lesbian travellers 150-1
LGBTQI+ travellers 150-1
Lighthouse 36
Lion Rock 111
Long Beach 131

M

Man O' War 101
Māori culture 17
McCahon House 111
mobile phones 151
money 24, 149-50, 151-2
Motubikes 106
Mt Eden 60-1
Mt Eden village 59-67, **62-3**
 drinking 66-7
 entertainment 67
 food 64-6

 shopping 67
 sights 60-1, 64
 transport 59
Muriwai 111-12
museums 17, 20

N

New Zealand Fashion Week 54
New Zealand Maritime Museum 53
Newmarket 69-79, **72-3**
 drinking 77-8
 entertainment 78
 food 75-7
 shopping 79
 sights 74-5
 transport 69
nightlife, see drinking & nightlife
Northland Paddleboarding 140

O

Oke Bay 131
Old Government House 36
Omata Estate 131
One Tree Hill 80-1
opening hours 149
Opua Forest 124

P

Paddles & Saddles 105
Paihia 119-27, **122**
 food 125-7
 shopping 127
 sights 120-1, 123-5
 transport 119
Parakai Springs 112
Parnell 69-79, **72-3**
 drinking 77-8
 shopping 79

 sights 70-1, 74-5
 transport 69
Parnell Baths 75
Parnell Rose Garden 74
Pasifika Festival 40
Phantom 123
Piha 111
Pompallier Mission 131
Ponsonby 83-95, **86-7**
 drinking 90-3
 entertainment 93-4
 food 88-90
 shopping 94-5
 sights 84-5
 transport 83
Ponsonby Central 84-5
Potiki Adventures 101
public holidays 152

R

R Tucker Thompson 123
Rainbow Falls 139
Rangitoto 43
Rewa's Village 139-40
ride-sharing 149
rugby 67
Russell 129-35, **130**
 food 133-5
 history 132
 shopping 135
 sights 131-3
 transport 129
Russell Museum 132
Russell Nature Walks 132

S

safety 152
She's a Lady 123

shopping 14-15, *see also individual neighbourhoods*, Shopping *subindex*
Silo Park 55
Sky Tower 38
SkyJump 38
SkyWalk 38
sports, *see* cricket, rugby, tennis
St Mary's Church 74
St Patrick's Cathedral 36
St Paul's Anglican Church 124
St Stephen's Chapel 74
Star Treks 105
Stardome 81
stargazing 106
Stonyridge 101
surfing 106

T

Taiamai Tours Heritage Journeys 123
Takapu Refuge gannet colony 111-12
Tamaki Drive 108-9
Tāmaki Hikoi 37
taxis 149
Te Henga (Bethells Beach) 16
Te Kōngahu Museum of Waitangi 121
Te Uru Waitakere Contemporary Gallery 111
telephone services 151
tennis 79
time 24
TIME Unlimited 111
tipping 152
Tiritiri Matangi 43
Titirangi 111
toilets 152

top sights 6-9
tourist information 152-3
tours 21
train travel 149
transport 25, 147-9
Treaty House 121
Twin Coast Cycle Trail 125

U

University Clock Tower 37
Urupukapuka Island 134

V

vegetarian travellers 40, 91
Viaduct Harbour 49-57, **52**
drinking 56-7
entertainment 57
food 54-6
itineraries 50-1, **50**
sights 53-4
transport 49
walks 50-1, **50**
visas 153
Volcanic Explorer 43
volcanoes 19

W

Waiheke Island 97-103, **100**
drinking 103
driving tours 98-9, **98**
food 102
itineraries 98-9, **98**
shopping 103
sights 101
transport 97
Waitākere Ranges 115

Waitangi Treaty Grounds 120-1
walks 57, *see also individual neighbourhoods*
weather 146
websites 146
West Auckland 110-15, **113**
Wharepuke Falls 139
Wild on Waiheke 101
Williams House & Gardens 124
Windy Canyon Lookout 106
wine 112, 140
Wintergarden 74
Wynyard Quarter 49-57, **52**
drinking 56-7
entertainment 57
food 54-6
itineraries 50-1, **50**
sights 53-4
transport 49
walks 50-1, **50**

✘ Eating

&Sushi 76

A

Acho 91
Ake Ake 141
Amano 39
Apero 89
Atomic Roastery 65-6
Auckland Fish Market 55-6
Azabu 88

B

Baduzzi 55
Bayside Restaurant & Bar 134

Bestie 90
Billy 71
Bird on a Wire 85
Black Olive 143
Blue Breeze Inn 85
Brothers Juke Joint BBQ 66
Burger Burger 85

C

Cafe Jerusalem 142
Cafe Zest & the Waffle Room 143
Casita Miro 102
Cassia 38
Charlotte's Kitchen 125
Chuffed 41
Cotto 88-9

D

Dairy 85
Dante's Pizza 85
Deco Eatery 111
Delish 135
Depot 39
Dragonfired 102
Duke of Marlborough Hotel 133-4

E

Ebisu 40
El Cafe 126
Ela Cuisine 42

F

Federal & Wolfe 40-1
Federal Delicatessen 41-2
Fort Greene 90
Frasers 64
French Cafe 64

G

Gables 133
Garden Shed 61
Gemmayze St 88
Gerome 75
Giapo 39
Giraffe 56
Good Luck Coconut 55
Greens 134-5
Grove 39
Gusto at the Grand 42

H

Hallertau 111, 115
Han 76
Hansan 77
Hello Beasty 54
Hōne's Garden 133

I

Ima 41
Island Gelato 102

K

Kimchi Project 40

L

La Cigale 76
Little & Friday 77
Little Bird Kitchen 90
Little Turkish Cafe 91
Lokanta 89-90
Lowbrow 91

M

Māha 142
Marsden Estate 142
Masu 39

Sights 000
Map Pages 000

Miss Istanbul 85
Morningside Precinct 65
My Fat Puku 105

N

Newport Chocolates 135

O

O'Connell Street Bistro 41
Old Packhouse Market 141
Ortolana 42

P

Pasta & Cuore 64
Pasture 75-6
Plough & Feather 141
Ponsonby Village International Food Court 85

R

Rasoi Vegetarian Restaurant 91
Revive 42
Rusty Tractor 141

S

Saan 88
Sage @ Paroa Bay 134
Saint Alice 55
Scarecrow 40
Sidart 88
St Heliers Bay Bistro 109

T

Tantalus Estate 102
Tasting Shed 115
Teed Street Larder 77
Terra 125

Three Seven Two 102
Tuk Tuk Bangkok 135

U

Uncle Man's 91

W

Whare Waka Cafe 125-6
Williams Eatery 54
Winona Forever 76-7
Woodpecker Hill 76

X

Xoong 65

Z

Zool Zool 64

🍷 Drinking

A

Ake Ake 141
Annabel's 92
Aotea Brewing 106
Auckland Wine Trail Tours 111

B

Bar Celeste 91
Bedford Soda & Liquor 85
Beer Spot 115
Brewers Co-operative 93
Brit, The 44
Brothers Beer 92

C

Caretaker 43-4
Citizen Park 67
Coopers Creek 112
Cottle Hill 140
Currach Irish Pub 106

D

Deadshot 90-1
Doolan Brothers 78
Dr Rudi's 56-7

F

Fine Wine Tours 111

G

Galbraith's Alehouse 66
Garage Project Cellar Door 66
Glasshouse Kitchen & Bar 127
Good George Craft House 109

H

Hallertau 111, 115
HI-SO 43
Hoppers Garden Bar 92
Hotel DeBrett 44-5

I

Island Coffee 103

J

Jefferson 45

K

Kumeu River 112

L

La Fuente 44
La Taza Del Diablo 143
Little Culprit 42
Lovebucket 91
Lumsden 77

M

Madame George 90
Mo's 43

P

Pineapple on Parnell 78
Portland Public House 67

S

Satya Chai Lounge 92-3
Sixteen Tun 56
Sofitel Auckland Viaduct Harbour 51
Soljans Estate 112

V

Vultures' Lane 44

W

Wine Cellar 93
Wynyard Pavilion 57

X

Xuxu 45

Z

Zane Grey's 126

✪ Entertainment

Academy Cinemas 45
Aotea Centre 47
ASB Tennis Centre 79
ASB Waterfront Theatre 57
Auckland Town Hall 46
Cathay Cinemas 143
Classic Comedy Club 46
Ding Dong Lounge 46
Eden Park 67
Neck of the Woods 94
Power Station 67
Q Theatre 46
Rialto 78
SkyCity Theatre 47
Whammy Bar 93

🛍 Shopping

Caravan Clothing & Home 135
Creative & Brave 79
Cross Street Market 94
Crushes 94-5
Flying Fish 127
Flying Out 95
Get Fudged & Keriblue Ceramics Studio 143
Huffer 79
Karen Walker 95
Kate Sylvester 79
Kura Gallery 57
Little Black Gallery 143
Makana Confections 143
Pauanesia 47
Poi Room 79
Real Groovy 47
Royal Jewellery Studio 67
South Sea Art 135
St Kevin's Arcade 94
Strangely Normal 47
Time Out 67
Unity Books 47
Waiheke Wine Centre 103
Westfield Newmarket 79
Women's Bookshop 95
Wood2Water 135
Zambesi 79, 95

159

Index

Our Writers

Brett Atkinson

Explore Auckland Brett Atkinson is based in Auckland, New Zealand, but frequently on the road for Lonely Planet. He's a full-time travel and food writer specialising in adventure travel, unusual destinations and surprising angles on better-known destinations. Craft beer and street food are Brett's favourite reasons to explore places, and he is featured regularly on the Lonely Planet website and in newspapers, magazines and websites across New Zealand and Australia. Since becoming a Lonely Planet author in 2005, Brett has covered areas as diverse as Vietnam, Sri Lanka, the Czech Republic, New Zealand, Morocco, California and the South Pacific. Brett also wrote the Plan Your Trip and Survival Guide chapters of this book.

Tasmin Waby

Explore the Bay of Islands London-born to Kiwi parents, Tasmin was raised in Australia, for which she is incredibly grateful. As well as travelling, learning and writing, Tasmin is madly in love with cartography, wild swimming and starry skies. When not on assignment she lives on a narrowboat in England, raising two hilariously funny school-age children and a fat Russian Blue cat called Millie.

Published by Lonely Planet Global Limited
CRN 554153
1st edition – February 2021
ISBN 978 1 78868 943 4
© Lonely Planet 2021 Photographs © as indicated 2021
10 9 8 7 6 5 4 3 2 1
Printed in Singapore

Although the authors and Lonely Planet have taken all reasonable care in preparing this book, we make no warranty about the accuracy or completeness of its content and, to the maximum extent permitted, disclaim all liability arising from its use.

All rights reserved. No part of this publication may be copied, stored in a retrieval system, or transmitted in any form by any means, electronic, mechanical, recording or otherwise, except brief extracts for the purpose of review, and no part of this publication may be sold or hired, without the written permission of the publisher. Lonely Planet and the Lonely Planet logo are trademarks of Lonely Planet and are registered in the US Patent and Trademark Office and in other countries. Lonely Planet does not allow its name or logo to be appropriated by commercial establishments, such as retailers, restaurants or hotels. Please let us know of any misuses: lonelyplanet.com/ip.